EDGARDO FERNANDEZ CLIMENT

CIS Controls in Practice

A Comprehensive Implementation Guide

Copyright © 2024 by Edgardo Fernandez Climent

All rights reserved. No part of this publication may be reproduced, stored or transmitted in any form or by any means, electronic, mechanical, photocopying, recording, scanning, or otherwise without written permission from the publisher. It is illegal to copy this book, post it to a website, or distribute it by any other means without permission.

Edgardo Fernandez Climent has no responsibility for the persistence or accuracy of URLs for external or third-party Internet Websites referred to in this publication and does not guarantee that any content on such Websites is, or will remain, accurate or appropriate.

Designations used by companies to distinguish their products are often claimed as trademarks. All brand names and product names used in this book and on its cover are trade names, service marks, trademarks and registered trademarks of their respective owners. The publishers and the book are not associated with any product or vendor mentioned in this book. None of the companies referenced within the book have endorsed the book.

First edition

*This book was professionally typeset on Reedsy.
Find out more at reedsy.com*

Contents

Preface	1
Why Cybersecurity Matters:	1
About CIS Controls	4
Chapter 1: Understanding CIS Controls	9
The Genesis of CIS Controls: From Critical Security Controls to Modern Framework	9
CIS Controls Overview: A Comprehensive Breakdown by Implementation Groups	13
Benefits and Challenges of Implementing CIS Controls	17
Chapter 2: Preparing for CIS Controls Implementation	22
Conducting Cybersecurity Posture Assessments for CIS Controls Implementation	22
Tailoring CIS Controls to Your Organization's Requirements	26
Developing a Strategic Implementation Roadmap for CIS Controls	31
Chapter 3: Assembling Your Cybersecurity Team	36
Defining Roles and Responsibilities for CIS Controls Implementation	36
Building and Training Your Cybersecurity Team for CIS Controls Implementation	40
Fostering Team Collaboration for Successful CIS Controls Implementation	45
Chapter 4: Implementing Enterprise Asset Controls (Controls...	50
Control 1: Inventory and Control of Enterprise Assets - Comprehensive Implementation Guide	50

Control 2: Inventory and Control of Software Assets- Comprehensive Implementation Guide ... 58
Control 3: Data Protection- Comprehensive Implementation Guide ... 67
Control 4: Secure Configuration of Enterprise Assets and Software- Comprehensive Implementation Guide ... 76
Chapter 5: Implementing Account and Access Management... 85
Control 5: Account Management- Comprehensive Implementation Guide ... 85
Control 6: Access Control Management- Comprehensive Implementation Guide ... 93
Chapter 6: Implementing Continuous Monitoring and Defense... 102
Control 7: Continuous Vulnerability Management- Comprehensive Implementation Guide ... 102
Control 8: Audit Log Management- Comprehensive Implementation Guide ... 110
Control 9: Email and Web Browser Protections- Comprehensive Implementation Guide ... 118
Control 10: Malware Defenses - Comprehensive Implementation Guide ... 127
Control 11: Data Recovery- Comprehensive Implementation Guide ... 136
Control 12: Network Infrastructure Management- Comprehensive Implementation Guide ... 145
Control 13: Network Monitoring and Defense- Comprehensive Implementation Guide ... 153
Control 14: Security Awareness and Skills Training- Comprehensive Implementation Guide ... 162
Chapter 7: Implementing Governance and Organizational... 172

Control 15: Service Provider Management- Comprehensive Implementation Guide	172
Control 16: Application Software Security- Comprehensive Implementation Guide	180
Control 17: Incident Response Management- Comprehensive Implementation Guide	188
Control 18: Penetration Testing- Comprehensive Implementation Guide	196
Chapter 8: Understanding and Applying Implementation Groups...	206
Introduction to Implementation Groups	206
Implementation Group 1 (IG1) - Basic Cyber Hygiene	210
Implementation Group 2 (IG2) - Intermediate Cyber Hygiene	214
Implementation Group 3 (IG3) - Advanced Cyber Defense	218
Determining Your Implementation Group	222
Moving Between Implementation Groups: Strategy and Execution	226
Implementation Group Best Practices	230
Implementation Group Case Studies and Real-World Examples	234
Chapter 9: Maintaining and Enhancing Your Cybersecurity...	239
Routine Assessments and Audits: Maintaining Security Effectiveness	239
Adapting to New Threats: Maintaining Security Effectiveness in a Dynamic Landscape	243
Leveraging Community Knowledge and Resources: Harnessing Collective Security Intelligence	247
Chapter 10: Navigating Implementation Challenges	251
Common Implementation Pitfalls and Their Solutions: A Practical Guide	251

Securing Executive Support and Funding: Building Leadership Commitment to Security — 255
Chapter 11: Future-Proofing Your Cybersecurity with CIS... — 260
    Adapting CIS Controls to Emerging Technologies and Trends — 260
    Scaling Security Strategies for Organizational Growth — 263
Chapter 12: Measuring Impact and Success — 268
    Key Performance Indicators (KPIs): Measuring Security Program Success — 268
    Comprehensive Security KPI Definitions — 272
    Return on Security Investment (ROSI): Understanding Security Value — 277
    Continuous Improvement Cycle: Maintaining and Enhancing Security Controls — 281
Closing — 285
    Key Takeaways: Critical Elements for Successful CIS Controls Implementation — 285
    The Journey Ahead: Maintaining Security Excellence — 289
Appendix A: Glossary of Cybersecurity Terms — 294
Appendix B: List of Acronyms with Explanations — 299
Appendix C: CIS Controls Implementation Resources — 308
Appendix D: Recommended Reading and Resources — 313
About the Author — 317
Also by Edgardo Fernandez Climent — 320

Preface

Why Cybersecurity Matters:

Cybersecurity has evolved from a specialized technical concern to a fundamental business imperative that touches every aspect of modern operations. The acceleration of digital transformation across industries has created unprecedented opportunities for innovation and efficiency. Still, it has also expanded the attack surface that organizations must defend against increasingly sophisticated threats.

The threat landscape of 2024 presents challenges that would have been difficult to imagine just a few years ago. State-sponsored cyber operations have become more prevalent, targeting not just government institutions but also private enterprises that form part of critical infrastructure and supply chains. Ransomware attacks have evolved from opportunistic campaigns to highly targeted operations, with threat actors conducting detailed reconnaissance to maximize leverage over their victims. The average data breach cost now exceeds $4.5 million, reflecting both the direct costs of incident response and the long-term impact on business operations and customer trust.

The proliferation of Internet of Things (IoT) devices has introduced new vulnerabilities into enterprise networks. These devices, often deployed with default credentials and irregular patch cycles, create persistent security gaps that sophisticated attackers can exploit. The rise of operational technology (OT) environments connecting to traditional IT networks has further complicated the security landscape, requiring organizations to protect systems never designed with cybersecurity in mind.

Cloud adoption has transformed the traditional security perimeter, rendering the notion of a clearly defined network boundary obsolete. Organizations must now secure dynamic, distributed environments where data and applications move freely between on-premises infrastructure, public cloud services, and employee devices. This shift has given rise to new attack vectors, as evidenced by the increasing frequency of cloud misconfiguration exploits and supply chain compromises.

The human element remains a critical factor in cybersecurity. Social engineering attacks have become more sophisticated, leveraging artificial intelligence to create convincing phishing campaigns and deepfake media that can deceive even security-conscious employees. The rise of remote work has expanded the attack surface, with home networks and personal devices becoming potential entry points for corporate network compromises.

Regulatory requirements around data protection and privacy have also evolved significantly. Organizations must now navigate a complex landscape of compliance requirements, from GDPR and CCPA to industry-specific regulations. The cost of non-compliance has increased substantially, with regulatory fines often exceeding the

PREFACE

direct costs of security incidents.

The cybersecurity skills gap continues to pose significant challenges for organizations. With millions of cybersecurity positions unfilled globally, organizations struggle to build and maintain the expertise to defend against modern threats. This shortage emphasizes the importance of implementing frameworks like CIS Controls to help organizations systematically approach security improvements, even with limited resources.

Small and medium-sized enterprises face particular challenges in this environment. While they may not have the resources of larger organizations, they face many of the same threats and are often targeted specifically because of their perceived vulnerabilities. The democratization of cyber attack tools through ransomware-as-a-service and other criminal enterprises has made sophisticated attack capabilities available to a broader range of threat actors.

The financial services sector has seen a sharp increase in targeted attacks, with threat actors exploiting the interconnected nature of modern financial systems. Healthcare organizations remain prime targets, with patient data and critical care systems presenting attractive targets for both cybercriminals and nation-state actors. The manufacturing and critical infrastructure sectors face growing threats from attacks designed to disrupt operations and compromise industrial control systems.

In this environment, a systematic approach to cybersecurity is not just desirable—it's essential for organizational survival. The CIS Controls provide a practical, prioritized path to improving security posture based on real-world attack data and proven defensive techniques. They offer a framework organizations can use to focus their limited resources on the most effective security measures, addressing common and sophisticated threats.

As we explore the CIS Controls throughout this book, we'll see how they address these modern challenges while remaining flexible enough to adapt to emerging threats. The controls provide a foundation for building robust security programs that can evolve with the threat landscape, helping organizations move from reactive security measures to proactive risk management.

The stakes in cybersecurity have never been higher, and the cost of inadequate security continues to grow. As we progress, the organizations that thrive will recognize cybersecurity as a strategic imperative and implement comprehensive security programs based on proven frameworks like the CIS Controls. The following chapters will provide the knowledge and practical guidance needed to implement these controls effectively, helping you build a more resilient security posture for your organization.

About CIS Controls

The Center for Internet Security (CIS) Controls has emerged as one of the most trusted and practical frameworks for organizations seeking to strengthen their cybersecurity posture. In version 8.1, these controls represent a distillation of decades of cybersecurity experience, offering organizations a prioritized pathway to improve their security against real-world threats.

PREFACE

The evolution of CIS Controls reflects the dynamic nature of the cybersecurity landscape. Originally developed by the National Security Agency (NSA) in response to significant data loss incidents at the U.S. Department of Defense, these controls have transformed through collaborative refinement by a global community of IT and security professionals. The transition from version 7.1 to version 8 marked a significant shift in approach, with version 8.1 further refining these changes to address modern technological environments.

Version 8.1 represents a fundamental reimagining of how organizations should approach cybersecurity. The controls have been reorganized to reflect the reality of modern enterprise environments, where cloud services, remote work, and mobile devices have blurred traditional network boundaries. The current 18 controls are carefully structured to address fundamental security needs and advanced threats, making them relevant for organizations of all sizes and complexity levels.

A key strength of CIS Controls v8.1 lies in its Implementation Groups (IGs). These groups recognize that not all organizations have the same resources or face the same threat levels. Implementation Group 1 (IG1) provides essential cyber hygiene measures suitable for small organizations. Implementation Group 2 (IG2) builds upon this foundation for organizations with more complex needs and resources. Implementation Group 3 (IG3) adds sophisticated controls for organizations requiring the highest level of security. This tiered approach allows organizations to implement security measures appropriate to their risk profile and resource capacity.

The technical depth of CIS Controls v8.1 becomes apparent in their implementation. Consider Control 1, "Inventory and Control of

Enterprise Assets." While this might sound straightforward, its technical implementation involves automated discovery tools, asset management databases, and continuous monitoring systems. The control provides specific guidance on implementing these technical solutions while maintaining the flexibility to accommodate various technological environments.

Modern cybersecurity strategies particularly benefit from the controls' emphasis on automation and continuous monitoring. Take Control 7, "Continuous Vulnerability Management," which outlines specific technical requirements for automated scanning, assessment, and remediation workflows. This approach acknowledges that manual processes can't keep pace with today's rapidly evolving threat landscape.

The controls also address the convergence of IT and operational technology (OT) environments. Manufacturing organizations, for instance, can use the controls to secure traditional IT and industrial control systems (ICS). The framework guides securing these specialized environments while maintaining operational reliability and safety requirements.

Cloud computing receives particular attention in v8.1. The controls have been updated to address cloud-specific security challenges, including identity and access management, data protection across multiple cloud services, and security monitoring in hybrid environments. This makes the controls especially relevant for organizations undergoing cloud transformation initiatives.

The practical value of CIS Controls becomes evident in their approach to security metrics and measurement. Each control includes specific metrics organizations can use to assess their security posture and demonstrate compliance to stakeholders. These metrics are designed to be actionable and meaningful, helping organizations track their security progress over time.

Integration with other security frameworks enhances the utility of CIS Controls. They align well with other standards such as NIST CSF, ISO 27001, and industry-specific regulations. This alignment helps organizations maintain compliance with multiple frameworks without duplicating efforts. For example, an organization implementing CIS Controls can map these efforts to NIST CSF requirements, streamlining compliance processes.

Their real-world application demonstrates the controls' effectiveness. Consider a manufacturing organization implementing Control 12, "Network Infrastructure Management." Following the control's guidance on network segmentation and secure configuration, they successfully prevented a ransomware attack from spreading from their corporate network to their production systems. This kind of practical success story validates the controls' real-world effectiveness.

The controls also address emerging technologies and threats. They guide the security of containerized environments, cloud-native applications, and DevOps pipelines. This forward-looking approach helps organizations secure not just their current infrastructure but also their future technology initiatives.

Looking ahead, CIS Controls continue to evolve with the threat landscape. The framework's community-driven development process ensures that it remains relevant and practical. Regular updates incorporate lessons learned from real-world security incidents and emerging attack patterns, making the controls a living document that reflects current best practices in cybersecurity.

The framework provides both strategic guidance and tactical recommendations for IT professionals implementing these controls. Each control includes specific technical requirements while maintaining flexibility in implementation approaches. This balance makes the controls particularly valuable for organizations that need to improve their security posture while working within operational constraints.

In subsequent chapters, we'll explore specific implementation strategies, common challenges, and practical solutions as we delve deeper into each control. The goal is to help you transform these controls from theoretical concepts into practical security improvements for your organization.

Chapter 1: Understanding CIS Controls

The Genesis of CIS Controls: From Critical Security Controls to Modern Framework

The story of CIS Controls begins in the late 2000s, emerging from a critical need to address widespread cyber attacks targeting defense industrial base companies. What started as a collaborative effort between the National Security Agency (NSA) and the Defense Industrial Base (DIB) has evolved into one of the most respected and widely adopted cybersecurity frameworks globally.

The initial catalyst came in 2008 when the Office of the Secretary of Defense asked the NSA's Information Assurance Directorate to develop a prioritized baseline of security controls. This request was driven by massive data losses occurring across defense contractors. The NSA's response was to analyze the most common attack patterns and develop countermeasures that would have prevented these breaches. This practical, data-driven approach became a defining characteristic of what would later become the CIS Controls.

The Consensus Audit Guidelines (CAG) framework was developed through intensive collaboration between government agencies and civilian organizations. These guidelines significantly shifted from traditional compliance-based security approaches to a threat-focused methodology. Rather than simply checking boxes for compliance, organizations could now focus on implementing controls that directly addressed real-world attacks.

By 2009, these guidelines had evolved into the Critical Security Controls (CSC), managed by the SANS Institute. This transition marked an important shift toward broader civilian adoption. The controls gained significant credibility when the U.S. State Department reported a 94% reduction in measured security risk through their implementation. This success story helped establish the controls as a practical framework for organizations beyond the defense sector.

The Center for Internet Security took over stewardship of the controls in 2015, marking another significant evolution. Under CIS leadership, the controls became more accessible to organizations of varying sizes and technical capabilities. The introduction of Implementation Groups in version 7 was a revolutionary change, acknowledging that not all organizations need to implement every control to achieve basic security hygiene.

The transition from version 7.1 to version 8 in 2021 represented the most significant restructuring in the framework's history. This update reflected fundamental changes in technology landscapes, particularly the shift to cloud computing and remote work environments. The previous 20 controls were consolidated into 18, with a stronger emphasis on cloud security, application security, and access management.

Version 8.1, released in 2023, further refined these changes while

CHAPTER 1: UNDERSTANDING CIS CONTROLS

maintaining the core principle of prioritizing security measures based on real-world attack data. This version enhanced guidance for cloud environments, mobile devices, and modern application architectures. The refinements reflected the growing complexity of enterprise technology environments and the need for more nuanced security controls.

Several key architectural changes marked the transition to v8.1. The controls were reorganized to align with modern enterprise architectures, where traditional network boundaries have dissolved. The framework better addresses security challenges in hybrid environments, where resources span on-premises data centers, cloud services, and edge computing platforms.

The evolution of Implementation Groups also reflects growing sophistication in how organizations approach security. IG1 now provides essential cyber hygiene measures suitable for smaller organizations with limited resources. IG2 adds controls for organizations with more complex environments and dedicated IT staff. IG3 provides comprehensive security measures for organizations requiring the highest level of security, such as those in regulated industries or handling sensitive data.

The technical depth of controls has increased significantly with each version. Early versions focused primarily on technical controls like firewalls and antivirus software. Version 8.1 now includes sophisticated guidance on container security, API protection, and cloud service configuration. This evolution reflects the increasing complexity of enterprise technology environments and the need for more comprehensive security measures.

Documentation and guidance have also evolved substantially. While early versions provided basic technical requirements, current documentation includes detailed implementation guidance, tool recommendations, and assessment procedures. This enhanced guidance helps organizations understand what to do and how to do it effectively.

The community-driven development process has become more sophisticated over time. The controls now benefit from input from a global community of security practitioners, incorporating lessons learned from real-world implementations and emerging threats. This collaborative approach ensures the controls remain practical and relevant to current security challenges.

The framework's relationship with other security standards has also evolved. Version 8.1 strongly aligns with frameworks like NIST CSF, ISO 27001, and various regulatory requirements. This alignment helps organizations leverage their CIS Controls implementation to demonstrate compliance with multiple standards, reducing duplicate effort and complexity.

Looking toward the future, CIS Controls continue to evolve in the threat landscape. The framework's development process now includes regular reviews of emerging technologies and threats, ensuring it remains relevant as technology advances. This forward-looking approach helps organizations prepare for future security challenges while addressing current needs.

The journey from the original Consensus Audit Guidelines to CIS Controls v8.1 reflects the maturing of the cybersecurity industry itself. What began as a focused effort to protect defense contractors has evolved into a comprehensive framework that helps organizations of all sizes build effective security programs. This evolution continues, driven by technological changes, emerging threats, and lessons learned from real-world implementations.

CIS Controls Overview: A Comprehensive Breakdown by Implementation Groups

The CIS Controls v8.1 framework comprises 18 distinct controls organized into three Implementation Groups. It provides a scalable approach to cybersecurity that adapts to an organization's size, resources, and security requirements. Understanding how these controls are structured across implementation groups is crucial for effective deployment.

Implementation Group 1 (IG1) forms the foundation of essential cyber hygiene, designed for organizations with limited resources and cybersecurity expertise. These basic safeguards protect against the most common cyber attacks while requiring minimal technical sophistication. Within IG1, organizations focus on fundamental security measures such as asset inventory, secure configurations, and basic access control.

The first key control in IG1 focuses on Enterprise **Asset Management**. Organizations maintain a basic inventory of physical devices connected to their network at this level. This doesn't require sophisticated automated tools—even a regularly updated spreadsheet can serve as a starting point. The goal is to ensure that no unknown devices can connect to the network, potentially compromising security.

Software Asset Management follows closely, requiring organizations to track authorized software installations. IG1 implementation might involve maintaining an approved software list and using basic endpoint protection to prevent unauthorized software installation. This control helps prevent malware infections and reduces the attack surface without requiring advanced technical capabilities.

Data Protection controls at the IG1 level emphasize basic data classification and storage practices. Organizations identify their sensitive data and implement fundamental protection measures such as encryption for data at rest and in transit. This might involve using built-in encryption features in operating systems and enabling secure protocols for data transmission.

Implementation Group 2 (IG2) builds upon these foundations, adding sophisticated controls for organizations with dedicated IT security resources. IG2 implementations typically involve more automated tools and advanced security measures. For instance, the **Enterprise Asset Management** control expands to include automated discovery tools and real-time asset tracking systems.

In IG2, the **Account Management** control becomes more robust, incorporating automated account provisioning systems and regular privilege audits. Organizations at this level implement role-based access control (RBAC) systems and maintain detailed logs of account activities. This might involve deploying identity management solutions that integrate with existing directory services.

Continuous Vulnerability Management takes on greater significance in IG2. Organizations implement regular automated scanning across their infrastructure, with structured processes for prioritizing and remediating discovered vulnerabilities. This often involves dedicated vulnerability management platforms integrated with ticketing systems for tracking remediation efforts.

Implementation Group 3 (IG3) represents the most comprehensive security posture, suitable for organizations handling sensitive data or operating in regulated industries. At this level, controls are implemented with sophisticated automation, advanced monitoring capabilities, and comprehensive security processes.

For example, the **Network Infrastructure Management** control in IG3 involves advanced network segmentation, sophisticated access controls, and continuous monitoring of network configurations. Organizations might implement software-defined networking (SDN) solutions with automated policy enforcement and real-time threat detection capabilities.

Audit Log Management at the IG3 level requires advanced security information and event management (SIEM) systems capable of correlating events across multiple data sources. Organizations implement automated log analysis tools with machine learning capabilities to detect anomalies and potential security incidents.

Email and Web Browser Protections in IG3 incorporate advanced threat protection features such as sandboxing suspicious attachments, real-time URL filtering, and sophisticated phishing detection mechanisms. This might involve implementing secure email gateways with advanced threat protection capabilities and browser isolation technologies.

The **Service Provider Management** control becomes particularly sophisticated in IG3, requiring comprehensive vendor risk assessment processes, continuous monitoring of service provider security postures, and detailed security requirements in service-level agreements. Organizations might implement vendor risk management platforms integrated with continuous monitoring capabilities.

Penetration Testing in IG3 involves regular, comprehensive assessments of security controls using advanced testing methodologies. Organizations conduct internal and external penetration tests, often employing red team exercises to simulate sophisticated attack scenarios.

Each implementation group builds upon the previous one, creating a natural progression path for organizations as they mature their security programs. For instance, an organization might start with basic asset inventory spreadsheets in IG1, progress to automated discovery tools in IG2, and ultimately implement real-time asset intelligence platforms in IG3.

The framework's flexibility allows organizations to implement controls at different levels based on their specific needs and risk profiles. Some controls might be implemented at an IG3 level, while others remain at IG1 or IG2, depending on the organization's priorities and resources.

Cross-cutting themes appear throughout all implementation groups, such as the emphasis on automation, continuous monitoring, and regular assessment of control effectiveness. However, the sophistication and comprehensiveness of these elements increase with each implementation group.

Authentication and authorization controls clearly demonstrate this progression. IG1 might implement basic password policies and user account management. IG2 adds multi-factor authentication and privileged access management. IG3 extends this further with advanced authentication mechanisms, behavioral analytics, and zero-trust architectures.

The success of CIS Controls implementation often depends on understanding what each control requires and how these requirements evolve across implementation groups. This allows organizations to plan their security journey effectively, implementing controls at appropriate levels while maintaining a clear path for future enhancement.

Benefits and Challenges of Implementing CIS Controls

Implementing CIS Controls offers organizations substantial benefits while presenting distinct challenges that require careful navigation. Understanding both aspects helps organizations prepare for successful implementation while setting realistic expectations for their security journey.

The primary benefit of implementing CIS Controls lies in their proven effectiveness against real-world threats. Organizations that successfully implement these controls often experience significant reductions in security incidents. A mid-sized manufacturing company, for instance, reported an 85% reduction in malware infections within six months of implementing just the basic IG1 controls. The framework's focus on addressing common attack patterns means that even partial implementation can yield substantial security improvements.

Cost reduction represents another significant advantage. Organizations can maximize their security investment return by prioritizing controls that address the most common attack vectors. A healthcare organization implementing CIS Controls discovered they could eliminate several redundant security tools, reducing their annual security spending by 30% while improving their overall security posture. The framework's structured approach helps organizations avoid purchasing security solutions without clearly understanding their value proposition.

CIS Controls implementation makes regulatory compliance more manageable. The controls align with major compliance frameworks, including HIPAA, PCI DSS, and GDPR. A financial services firm found that their CIS Controls implementation satisfied approximately 70% of their PCI DSS requirements, streamlining their compliance efforts. This alignment reduces the overhead of maintaining multiple compliance programs and simplifies audit preparations.

Improved incident response capabilities emerge naturally from proper implementation. Organizations gain better visibility into their security posture and can detect and respond to threats more effectively. A technology company detected and contained a potential data breach within hours rather than days after implementing Control 8 (Audit Log Management) and Control 13 (Network Monitoring and Defense), potentially saving millions in breach-related costs.

However, organizations face several significant challenges during implementation. **Resource constraints often top the list of implementation obstacles.** Many organizations struggle to allocate sufficient staff time and budget for implementation. A retail company initially attempted to implement all controls simultaneously, leading to project stagnation. They succeeded only after adopting a phased approach, focusing first on IG1 controls and gradually progressing to more advanced measures.

Technical complexity presents another substantial challenge. Organizations frequently underestimate the technical prerequisites for certain controls. A manufacturing firm attempted to implement Control 7 (Continuous Vulnerability Management) without establishing proper asset inventory and configuration management. This led to incomplete scanning coverage and false positives that overwhelmed their security team. Success came only after they stepped back to properly implement Controls 1 and 2 as a foundation.

Organizational resistance often emerges during implementation. Business units may resist changes that they perceive as obstacles to productivity. A software development company faced significant pushback when implementing Control 6 (Access Control Management) because developers felt it would slow down their work. The solution involved careful communication of security benefits and gradual implementation that balanced security needs with operational efficiency.

Legacy systems pose particular challenges for CIS Controls implementation. Many organizations maintain critical systems that cannot easily be updated or reconfigured to meet control requirements. A utility company struggled with Control 4 (Secure Configuration of Enterprise Assets and Software) because of legacy SCADA systems. They succeeded by implementing compensating controls and additional network segmentation to protect vulnerable legacy systems.

Integration with existing processes and tools can be complex. Organizations often maintain various security tools that don't communicate effectively with each other. A government agency struggled to implement Control 8 (Audit Log Management) because their existing tools generated logs in different formats and stored them in separate locations. They ultimately implemented a SIEM solution with custom log parsers to achieve centralized log management.

Cultural challenges frequently arise during implementation. Security awareness and training programs often face resistance or apathy. A professional services firm initially struggled with Control 14 (Security Awareness and Skills Training) because employees viewed training as a checkbox exercise. Success came after they redesigned their training program to include relevant, role-specific scenarios and regular phishing simulations.

Change management proves crucial yet challenging during implementation. Organizations must carefully balance security improvements with operational continuity. A healthcare provider initially faced service disruptions when implementing Control 12 (Network Infrastructure Management) because of insufficient testing and communication. They succeeded after developing a robust change management process that included thorough testing and stakeholder communication.

Documentation and process maintenance present ongoing challenges. Organizations often struggle to keep security documentation current as their environments evolve. A technology company addressed this by implementing a documentation review cycle aligned with their quarterly business reviews, ensuring security documentation remained current and relevant.

Despite these challenges, organizations can achieve successful

implementation through careful planning and realistic expectations. Success often comes from starting with fundamental controls and progressively building more sophisticated security measures. A manufacturing company achieved significant security improvements by focusing initially on IG1 controls and expanding their implementation over two years as their security program matured.

The key to overcoming these challenges is approaching implementation as a journey rather than a destination. Organizations should focus on continuous improvement rather than perfect implementation. Regular assessment and adjustment of control implementation helps organizations maintain security effectiveness while adapting to changing business needs and emerging threats.

Chapter 2: Preparing for CIS Controls Implementation

Conducting Cybersecurity Posture Assessments for CIS Controls Implementation

Before implementing CIS Controls, organizations must accurately assess their current cybersecurity posture to determine the appropriate Implementation Group (IG). This crucial first step ensures that security investments align with organizational capabilities and requirements.

A comprehensive cybersecurity posture assessment begins with evaluating five key organizational characteristics: size, data sensitivity, regulatory requirements, technical capabilities, and available resources. The interplay between these factors helps determine whether an organization should begin with IG1, advance to IG2, or pursue the comprehensive security measures of IG3.

Size assessment extends beyond simple employee counts. A technology startup with fifty employees might handle more sensitive data and face more sophisticated threats than a manufacturing company with five hundred employees. Consider a mid-sized healthcare provider that initially assumed it belonged in IG1 based on employee count alone. After assessing its data sensitivity and regulatory requirements, it correctly identified itself as an IG2 organization due to its handling of protected health information.

Data sensitivity evaluation requires careful analysis of data types, storage locations, and processing methods. A financial services firm conducting its assessment discovered that while its customer transaction data required IG3-level controls, its marketing systems could operate effectively under IG1 controls. This realization led to a hybrid implementation approach that optimized resource allocation while maintaining appropriate security levels.

Technical capability assessment demands an honest evaluation of your IT team's expertise and capacity. A manufacturing company initially attempted IG2 implementation but struggled to deploy advanced security tools. They succeeded only after reassessing their capabilities and starting with IG1 while simultaneously developing their team's technical skills through targeted training programs.

Resource availability analysis must consider both financial and human resources. A retail organization learned this lesson when it attempted to implement IG2 controls without adequate staffing. Its successful implementation came only after right-sizing its approach to match available resources, starting with IG1 controls and gradually expanding its security team's capabilities.

The assessment process should examine current security controls against CIS benchmarks. A technology company used the CIS-CAT Pro Assessor tool to evaluate its systems against CIS Benchmarks, revealing significant gaps in its server configurations. This automated assessment provided concrete data for determining its implementation starting point.

Network architecture review forms another crucial assessment component. During its assessment, a professional services firm discovered that its flat network architecture would complicate the implementation of higher-level controls. This insight led them to prioritize network segmentation as an early implementation step, creating a foundation for more advanced security measures.

Application portfolio analysis helps identify security requirements across different systems. A government agency discovered during its assessment that while its public-facing applications required IG3 controls, its internal administrative systems could operate effectively under IG2 controls. This understanding helped it allocate security resources more efficiently.

Security incident history provides valuable insight for implementation group selection. A manufacturing company analyzing its incident history found that most security events resulted from basic security gaps addressable by IG1 controls. This data helped them resist pressure to immediately pursue more advanced controls before establishing fundamental security measures.

Vendor relationships and supply chain considerations impact implementation group selection. During its assessment, a healthcare technology company realized that despite its relatively small size, its role as a service provider to hospitals required it to implement IG3 controls. Thus, its customers' compliance requirements effectively determined its implementation group.

Regulatory compliance requirements often influence implementation group selection. During their assessment, a financial services provider discovered that their compliance obligations aligned closely with IG2 controls. This alignment helped them build a business case for the necessary security investments.

The assessment should also evaluate organizational culture and change readiness. During its assessment, a software development company recognized that its rapid development culture would challenge certain control implementations. This insight led to the development of change management strategies before beginning implementation.

Infrastructure complexity assessment helps determine implementation feasibility. A retail organization discovered during its assessment that its hybrid cloud environment would require additional planning for control implementation. This understanding helped them develop a phased approach that appropriately addressed cloud and on-premises environments.

Documentation review reveals gaps in existing security policies and procedures. A manufacturing firm found during its assessment that while it had many security controls in place, poor documentation would hinder implementation verification. This discovery led it to prioritize documentation improvement as part of its implementation strategy.

The assessment process should produce actionable findings. A technology services company organized its assessment results into immediate actions, short-term goals, and long-term objectives. This structured approach helped it develop a realistic implementation roadmap aligned with its capabilities and resources.

Regular reassessment ensures continued alignment between security controls and organizational needs. A healthcare provider established quarterly review cycles to evaluate their implementation progress and adjust their approach based on changing requirements and capabilities. This dynamic approach helped them maintain effective security controls while adapting to organizational growth.

Success in CIS Controls implementation often correlates directly with assessment quality. Organizations that conduct thorough initial assessments typically experience smoother implementations and achieve better security outcomes than those that rush into implementation without adequate preparation.

Tailoring CIS Controls to Your Organization's Requirements

Successfully implementing CIS Controls requires thoughtful adaptation to your organization's unique environment, requirements, and constraints. While the controls provide a robust security framework, their effectiveness depends on how well they're tailored to address specific organizational needs while maintaining security integrity.

The foundational principle of tailoring CIS Controls lies in understanding that security must support, not impede, business operations. Consider a software development company that needed to implement Control 5 (Account Management) in its DevOps environment. Rather than applying blanket restrictions that would slow development cycles, it adapted the control by implementing automated account provisioning integrated with its CI/CD pipeline, maintaining security while preserving development velocity.

Risk assessment plays a crucial role in control adaptation. A healthcare organization discovered that its legacy medical devices couldn't support standard endpoint protection solutions specified in Control 10 (Malware Defenses). Instead of forcing incompatible security measures, it developed compensating controls, including enhanced network segmentation and behavioral monitoring, to protect these critical systems while maintaining patient care capabilities.

Technical environment considerations significantly influence control implementation. A manufacturing company operating IT and OT networks found that standard vulnerability scanning approaches specified in Control 7 (Continuous Vulnerability Management) could disrupt sensitive industrial control systems. They adapted the control by implementing passive vulnerability assessment techniques for OT environments while maintaining active scanning in IT networks.

Resource constraints often necessitate creative adaptation. A mid-sized retail organization lacked the budget for enterprise-grade security information and event management (SIEM) systems specified in Control 8 (Audit Log Management). They developed an effective alternative using open-source tools and custom scripts to aggregate and analyze security logs, meeting the control's intent while working within their budget constraints.

Regulatory requirements must be considered when tailoring controls. A financial services provider needed to align CIS Controls with PCI DSS requirements. They mapped control modifications to specific compliance requirements, ensuring their adaptations satisfied security and regulatory needs. This mapping helped them identify areas where controls needed strengthening to meet compliance requirements.

Cloud adoption requires specific control adaptations. A technology company implementing Control 4 (Secure Configuration of Enterprise Assets and Software) realized that its traditional configuration management approach wouldn't work effectively in its cloud environment. It adapted the control by implementing infrastructure as code and automated compliance checking, maintaining security while leveraging cloud-native capabilities.

Business processes impact control implementation strategies. A professional services firm found that standard USB device restrictions specified in Control 1 (Enterprise Asset Management) conflicted with client presentation requirements. They modified the control by implementing USB allowlisting and automated malware scanning, balancing security needs with business functionality.

Geographic distribution affects control adaptation. A global manufacturing organization discovered that standard network monitoring approaches specified in Control 13 (Network Monitoring and Defense) couldn't effectively cover all their locations. They adapted the control by implementing a distributed monitoring architecture with regional collection points, maintaining comprehensive coverage while managing bandwidth constraints.

Industry-specific requirements influence control modification. A healthcare provider adapting Control 3 (Data Protection) needed to ensure rapid access to patient data in emergencies. They modified the control by implementing role-based emergency access procedures

CHAPTER 2: PREPARING FOR CIS CONTROLS IMPLEMENTATION

with automated auditing, maintaining data protection while ensuring patient care wasn't compromised.

Organizational culture shapes control implementation. A technology startup found that rigid access control policies specified in Control 6 (Access Control Management) conflicted with their collaborative culture. They adapted the control by implementing dynamic access controls based on project requirements, maintaining security while preserving workplace flexibility.

Technology stack considerations drive control customization. A software company using microservices architecture realized that traditional application security approaches specified in Control 16 (Application Software Security) weren't optimal for their environment. They adapted the control by implementing service mesh security controls and automated security testing in their deployment pipeline.

Third-party relationships affect control adaptation. A retailer working with numerous vendors found that standard vendor management approaches specified in Control 15 (Service Provider Management) were too rigid for their diverse supplier base. They modified the control by implementing tiered vendor requirements based on data access levels and integration depth.

Operational tempo influences control implementation. A news media organization needed to modify Control 9 (Email and Web Browser Protections) to accommodate rapid information-gathering needs. They adapted the control by implementing selective browser isolation technology, maintaining security while preserving operational agility.

Change management requirements shape control modification. A financial services firm found that standard change control processes specified in Control 12 (Network Infrastructure Management) were too slow for their trading operations. They adapted the control by implementing automated change verification and rollback capabilities, maintaining security while supporting operational requirements.

Measurement and validation must adapt alongside controls. A technology services provider realized standard security metrics wouldn't effectively measure their adapted controls. They developed custom metrics aligned with their modified implementation while maintaining the ability to demonstrate control effectiveness.

Documentation requirements change with control adaptation. A manufacturing company found standard security documentation approaches didn't effectively capture control modifications. They implemented a documentation system that tracked control adaptations and their rationale, maintaining transparency and auditability.

Success in tailoring CIS Controls requires maintaining each control's security intent while adapting its implementation details to organizational realities. Regularly reviewing and adjusting adapted controls ensures they provide effective security as organizational needs evolve.

CHAPTER 2: PREPARING FOR CIS CONTROLS IMPLEMENTATION

Developing a Strategic Implementation Roadmap for CIS Controls

Successful implementation of CIS Controls requires careful planning and a well-structured roadmap that accounts for organizational priorities, resource constraints, and technical dependencies. This strategic planning helps organizations avoid common pitfalls and ensures sustainable security improvements.

The foundation of effective implementation planning begins with baseline assessment results. A manufacturing company leveraged its initial assessment findings to identify quick wins and critical gaps, allowing it to prioritize its implementation efforts effectively. They discovered that implementing basic asset inventory controls would provide immediate visibility improvements while laying the groundwork for more advanced security measures.

Timeline development requires careful consideration of technical dependencies. A healthcare provider learned this lesson when they attempted to implement advanced log analysis capabilities before establishing proper log collection mechanisms. Their revised planning approach recognized that Control 8 (Audit Log Management) required fundamental logging infrastructure before advanced analysis could be effective.

Resource allocation planning must account for both implementation and ongoing maintenance needs. A financial services firm initially underestimated the staff time required for maintaining new security controls. Their successful implementation came after revising their resource plans to include dedicated control maintenance and tuning time, preventing security degradation over time.

Technical skill requirements should be mapped against current capabilities. A technology company developing its implementation roadmap identified specific training needs for different controls. They integrated skill development into their timeline, ensuring their team would be prepared for each implementation phase. This included scheduling targeted training sessions before implementing complex controls like continuous vulnerability management.

The definition of a milestone requires a balance between ambition and feasibility. A retail organization initially set aggressive implementation timeframes that proved unrealistic. Their revised approach established incremental milestones focused on foundational controls, with each success building momentum for subsequent implementations. They found that achieving smaller milestones regularly maintained project momentum better than pursuing larger, more time-consuming objectives.

Stakeholder communication planning proves crucial for implementation success. A professional services firm developed a comprehensive communication strategy that informed business units about upcoming changes and their potential operational impacts. This proactive communication helped reduce resistance to security changes and enabled better coordination of implementation activities.

Budget planning must consider both direct and indirect costs. A manufacturing organization discovered hidden costs related to system upgrades required for certain controls. Their revised budget included contingency funds for unexpected technical requirements and accounted for potential productivity impacts during implementation.

CHAPTER 2: PREPARING FOR CIS CONTROLS IMPLEMENTATION

Risk management integration ensures security improvements align with business priorities. A financial services provider mapped their implementation timeline against risk assessment results, prioritizing controls addressing their most significant vulnerabilities. This risk-based approach helped justify resource allocation and maintained focus on high-impact security improvements.

Technical environment planning must account for system interdependencies. A healthcare organization discovered that implementing network segmentation affected multiple business applications. Their revised implementation plan included detailed technical impact analysis phases before major infrastructure changes, preventing unexpected service disruptions.

Change management requirements significantly influence implementation timing. A technology company integrated its security control implementation schedule with its standard change management windows, reducing business disruption and improving implementation success rates. This coordination proved especially important for controls affecting critical business systems.

Testing requirements must be incorporated into implementation timelines. A retail organization learned to include adequate testing phases for each control implementation, particularly for controls affecting customer-facing systems. Their approach included staging environments for testing control configurations before production deployment.

Documentation planning ensures proper knowledge transfer and maintenance capabilities. A manufacturing firm incorporated documentation requirements into its implementation timeline, allocating specific resources for maintaining technical documentation and updating security procedures. This investment in documentation proved valuable for both audit compliance and staff training.

Compliance deadline considerations often influence implementation prioritization. A healthcare provider aligned its implementation timeline with upcoming regulatory audit schedules, ensuring critical compliance-related controls received appropriate priority. This alignment helped it maintain compliance while progressing through its broader security improvement program.

Tool selection and deployment planning require careful coordination. A technology services company discovered that proper tool implementation often required more time than initially estimated. Their revised planning approach included pilots and proof-of-concept phases for major tool deployments, reducing implementation risks.

The definition of success metrics helps track implementation progress effectively. A financial services organization developed specific metrics for each implementation phase, helping them demonstrate progress to stakeholders and identify areas needing additional attention. These metrics evolved as their implementation progressed, reflecting increasing security maturity.

Periodic review points must be built into the implementation timeline. A manufacturing company scheduled quarterly review sessions to assess implementation progress and adjust its roadmap based on changing business requirements and lessons learned. These reviews helped the company maintain momentum while ensuring its security improvements remained aligned with business needs.

The implementation roadmap should remain flexible enough to accommodate changing priorities. A healthcare provider built adjustment periods into their timeline, allowing them to respond to new regulatory requirements without derailing their overall implementation progress. This flexibility proved crucial for maintaining long-term implementation success.

Chapter 3: Assembling Your Cybersecurity Team

Defining Roles and Responsibilities for CIS Controls Implementation

Implementing CIS Controls requires a well-structured team with clearly defined roles and responsibilities. The complexity of modern security programs demands specialized expertise across multiple domains, making it crucial to establish clear accountability and authority lines within the cybersecurity team structure.

The **Security Program Manager** is the cornerstone of CIS Controls implementation, orchestrating the security strategy and ensuring alignment with business objectives. This role in a financial services organization proved critical in translating technical security requirements into business-relevant initiatives. The Program Manager maintained oversight of implementation progress while coordinating with various stakeholders to ensure security measures supported rather than hindered business operations.

Security architecture plays a foundational role in implementing CIS

Controls. The **Security Architect** designs the overall security infrastructure that enables effective control implementation. A manufacturing company's Security Architect developed a comprehensive security architecture that facilitates proper network segmentation, access control, and monitoring capabilities. This role requires deep technical knowledge and an understanding of business processes and requirements.

Network Security Engineers focus on implementing controls related to network infrastructure and monitoring. Their responsibilities encompass network segmentation, firewall management, and intrusion detection systems. A healthcare organization's Network Security Engineers implemented Control 12 (Network Infrastructure Management) by designing and deploying network zones that separated clinical systems from administrative networks while maintaining necessary communication paths.

System Security Engineers handle endpoint security and system hardening requirements. In a technology company, these engineers developed and maintained secure configuration baselines for various operating systems and applications, directly supporting Control 4 (Secure Configuration of Enterprise Assets and Software). They work closely with system administrators to ensure security measures remain effective while supporting operational requirements.

Identity and Access Management Specialists focus on implementing Controls 5 and 6, managing user accounts and access permissions. A financial services provider's IAM team implemented role-based access control systems and privileged access management solutions, ensuring appropriate access levels while maintaining security. This role requires a deep understanding of authentication technologies and identity management frameworks.

Security Operations Center (SOC) Analysts provide continuous monitoring and incident response capabilities. In a retail organization, SOC analysts implemented Control 13 (Network Monitoring and Defense) by establishing 24/7 security monitoring and developing incident response procedures. They serve as the first line of defense against security threats, requiring strong analytical skills and incident-handling expertise.

Vulnerability Management Specialists focus on implementing Control 7 (Continuous Vulnerability Management). A technology services company's vulnerability management team established systematic processes for identifying, assessing, and remediating security vulnerabilities across the enterprise. This role requires expertise in vulnerability scanning tools and risk assessment methodologies.

Data Security Specialists concentrate on implementing Control 3 (Data Protection). These specialists developed and implemented data classification schemes, encryption standards, and data handling procedures in a healthcare organization. They work closely with business units to understand data flows and protection requirements while ensuring compliance with regulatory requirements.

Application Security Engineers focus on implementing Control 16 (Application Software Security). A software development company's AppSec team integrated security testing into the development pipeline and established secure coding standards. This role requires an understanding of security principles and software development practices.

Security Compliance Analysts ensure alignment between CIS Controls implementation and regulatory requirements. A financial services firm's compliance analysts map control implementations to various regulatory frameworks, ensuring security measures satisfy multiple compliance requirements simultaneously. They also maintain documentation and evidence of control effectiveness for audit purposes.

Security Training Specialists implement Control 14 (Security Awareness and Skills Training). A manufacturing organization's training specialist developed role-specific security training programs and measured their effectiveness through various metrics. This role requires both security knowledge and adult education expertise.

Vendor Risk Management Specialists implement Control 15 (Service Provider Management). A healthcare provider's vendor management team developed assessment frameworks and monitoring processes for third-party security risks. They work closely with procurement teams to ensure security requirements are properly incorporated into vendor agreements.

Technical Project Managers coordinate specific control implementation initiatives. For example, a retail organization's project managers maintain implementation schedules, coordinate resources, and manage dependencies between different control implementations. They serve as the bridge between technical teams and program management.

Security Engineering Support provides specialized expertise for specific security technologies. These engineers managed security tools and platforms in a technology company, ensuring proper configuration and integration. They often work across multiple control implementations, providing technical expertise where needed.

Each role requires a clear definition of authority and decision-making capabilities. A manufacturing firm established a RACI matrix for their security team, clearly defining who is responsible, accountable, consultable, and informed for various security activities. This clarity proved essential for effective control implementation and ongoing maintenance.

The effectiveness of these roles depends heavily on proper interaction and collaboration. A financial services provider established regular coordination meetings between different security roles, ensuring a consistent approach to control implementation across the organization. These interactions help maintain security program coherence while effectively leveraging diverse expertise.

Success in implementing CIS Controls often depends on recognizing when roles need adjustment based on organizational changes. A healthcare organization regularly reviewed and updated role definitions as its security program matured, ensuring its team structure continued to support effective security operations.

Building and Training Your Cybersecurity Team for CIS Controls Implementation

Building and training an effective cybersecurity team for CIS Controls implementation requires a strategic approach that balances technical expertise with practical experience. Organizations must develop comprehensive recruitment and training strategies addressing immediate implementation needs and long-term security program sustainability.

Recruitment strategy development begins with accurate skill gap analysis. A technology company conducted a detailed assessment of its existing team's capabilities against CIS Controls requirements, revealing specific expertise gaps in areas such as vulnerability management and security architecture. This analysis helped the company prioritize hiring efforts and develop targeted job descriptions aligned with its implementation needs.

Technical skill requirements vary significantly across different control domains. A financial services organization developed role-specific technical requirements based on the controls each position would implement. Vulnerability management positions require expertise in scanning tools and remediation processes. They sought experience with enterprise security frameworks and cloud security architectures for security architecture roles.

Industry experience often proves as valuable as technical certifications. A healthcare provider found that candidates with industry experience could more effectively implement controls in their regulated environment. Their revised recruitment strategy balanced technical expertise with industry knowledge, leading to more successful implementations that properly addressed sector-specific challenges.

Internal talent development offers significant advantages for building security teams. A manufacturing organization implemented a security career development program that identified promising IT staff and provided them with security training and mentoring opportunities. This approach helped them build a security team that understood their technical environment and business operations.

Certification requirements should align with specific role responsi-

bilities. A retail company mapped required certifications to different security roles, requiring CISSP certification for security architects while emphasizing practical certifications like Security+ for junior security analysts. This structured approach ensured team members possessed relevant theoretical knowledge while maintaining practical implementation capabilities.

Training program development requires careful consideration of both technical and operational needs. A technology services company developed a multi-tier training program that combined vendor-specific technical training with broader security concept education. Their program included hands-on labs where team members could practice implementing controls in a safe environment before working on production systems.

Knowledge transfer mechanisms prove crucial for team development. A financial services firm established a mentoring program where experienced security professionals guided newer team members through control implementations. This approach accelerated skill development while ensuring consistent implementation approaches across the organization.

Cross-training initiatives help build more resilient security teams. A healthcare organization implemented regular rotation programs where team members gained experience with different control implementations. This approach improved their team's flexibility and reduced key person dependencies while broadening individual skill sets.

Technical documentation training ensures proper knowledge management. A manufacturing firm developed training modules focused on creating and maintaining security documentation. This investment improved their ability to maintain consistent control implementations and simplified knowledge transfer when team changes occurred.

Vendor relationship management training proves essential for modern security teams. A retail organization developed training programs to manage security vendors and cloud service providers effectively. This training helped their team better implement Control 15 (Service Provider Management) while maximizing value from security investments.

Incident response training requires regular practical exercises. A technology company conducted monthly tabletop exercises, during which team members practiced responding to various security scenarios. These exercises helped identify training gaps while improving team coordination during security incidents.

Communication skills development often proves as important as technical training. A financial services provider included presentation and stakeholder communication modules in their security training program. This investment helped their security team more effectively advocate for resources and explain technical requirements to business stakeholders.

Project management training supports effective control implementation. A healthcare organization provided project management training to its technical security leads, improving their ability to plan and execute control implementations while effectively managing stakeholder expectations.

Performance measurement frameworks help identify training needs.

A manufacturing company developed specific performance metrics for different security roles, using these measurements to identify areas where additional training would improve implementation effectiveness. This data-driven approach helped them optimize their training investments.

Continuous learning programs maintain team effectiveness. A technology services provider established a security learning library and allocated specific time for team members to pursue professional development. This commitment to ongoing education helped their team stay current with evolving threats and security technologies.

Training effectiveness assessment requires regular review and adjustment. A financial services organization established quarterly reviews of their training programs, adjusting content and delivery methods based on implementation results and team feedback. This iterative approach helped maintain training relevance and effectiveness.

Budget considerations must balance immediate training needs with long-term development goals. A healthcare provider allocated their training budget across different time horizons, ensuring resources for immediate implementation needs and longer-term skill development. This structured approach helped them maintain consistent progress in team capability development.

Success in building and training security teams often depends on creating a culture of continuous improvement. Organizations emphasizing ongoing learning and professional development achieve better implementation results and maintain more stable security teams.

Fostering Team Collaboration for Successful CIS Controls Implementation

Effective collaboration within cybersecurity teams forms the cornerstone of successful CIS Controls implementation. The interconnected nature of modern security controls requires seamless coordination between technical specialists, business units, and stakeholders to achieve comprehensive security improvements.

Cross-functional collaboration begins with establishing clear communication channels. A technology company implemented a structured communication framework in which security architects regularly engaged with network engineers, system administrators, and application developers. This framework facilitated early identification of potential implementation challenges and improved solution development. Regular technical working groups provided forums for different specialists to share insights and coordinate their efforts.

Technical knowledge sharing proves essential for maintaining implementation momentum. A financial services organization established weekly technical deep-dive sessions where team members presented specific control implementations and discussed challenges they encountered. These sessions helped spread technical knowledge across the team while identifying opportunities for implementation improvements. The presentations were recorded and maintained in a knowledge base, creating valuable reference material for future implementations.

Collaborative tool selection significantly impacts team effectiveness. A healthcare provider carefully evaluated different collaboration platforms before selecting integrated tools with their existing workflows. They implemented a unified platform that combined project management, documentation sharing, and real-time communication capabilities. This integrated approach reduced communication overhead and improved coordination between different security functions.

Documentation collaboration requires specific attention. A manufacturing organization implemented a collaborative documentation system where multiple team members could update technical procedures and implementation guides simultaneously. They established clear documentation standards and review processes, ensuring consistency while enabling rapid knowledge sharing. This system proved particularly valuable during complex control implementations that affected multiple systems.

Incident response collaboration demands special consideration. A retail company developed collaborative incident response procedures that clearly defined roles and communication paths during security events. Regular practice exercises helped team members understand their responsibilities while building trust between different technical specialists. These exercises often revealed opportunities to improve both technical controls and team coordination.

Cross-team dependencies require careful management. A technology services provider implemented dependency mapping processes where different technical teams documented their interconnections and requirements. This mapping helped them schedule implementations more effectively while reducing unexpected impacts on business operations. Regular cross-team planning sessions helped maintain awareness of these dependencies and adjust implementation approaches accordingly.

Metrics sharing promotes collaborative improvement. A financial services firm developed shared dashboards showing implementation progress and control effectiveness across different security domains. These dashboards helped teams identify areas where collaboration could improve overall security effectiveness. Regular review sessions focused on these metrics helped maintain alignment between security functions.

Virtual collaboration capabilities prove increasingly important. A global manufacturing company established effective virtual collaboration practices that enabled security teams across different time zones to work together effectively. They implemented follow-the-sun support models for critical security functions while maintaining consistent implementation approaches across regions. Regular virtual team meetings helped maintain personal connections despite physical distance.

Conflict resolution mechanisms support healthy collaboration. A healthcare organization established clear processes for resolving technical disagreements between different specialists. These processes emphasized evidence-based decision-making while respecting different technical perspectives. Regular retrospective sessions helped teams learn from past conflicts and improve their collaborative approaches.

Knowledge retention strategies support long-term collaboration. A technology company implemented structured knowledge transfer processes where departing team members documented their specific expertise and implementation experiences. This documentation helped maintain implementation continuity while reducing the impact of staff changes. Regular knowledge-sharing sessions helped distribute this expertise across the team.

Collaborative testing improves implementation quality. A financial services provider established joint testing procedures where different technical specialists worked together to validate control implementations. These collaborative testing sessions often identified potential issues early in the implementation process, reducing production impacts. The sessions also helped build mutual understanding between different technical domains.

Team building activities support technical collaboration. A manufacturing firm incorporated regular team activities focused on building trust and understanding between different security specialists. These activities helped create personal connections that improved day-to-day technical collaboration. Regular informal discussion sessions allowed team members to share challenges and seek colleague support.

Leadership support proves crucial for maintaining collaborative environments. A retail organization's security leadership actively promoted collaboration by recognizing and rewarding effective team efforts. They established clear expectations for collaboration while providing the resources necessary for effective team coordination. Regular leadership engagement helped maintain focus on collaborative approaches to security improvements.

Cultural considerations significantly impact collaboration effectiveness. A technology services company worked to develop a culture where knowledge sharing was valued and rewarded. They encouraged team members to seek input from colleagues and share their expertise freely. This cultural focus helped create an environment where collaboration became natural rather than forced.

**Success in fostering team collaboration often depends on consis-

tently focusing on collaborative practices. Organizations that actively promote and support collaboration typically achieve better implementation results and maintain more effective security programs over time. Regular evaluation of collaborative practices helps identify improvement opportunities while ensuring collaboration continues to support security objectives effectively.

Chapter 4: Implementing Enterprise Asset Controls (Controls 1-4)

Control 1: Inventory and Control of Enterprise Assets - Comprehensive Implementation Guide

Control Overview

Control 1 establishes foundational asset management capabilities by actively tracking and managing all enterprise assets with network access capabilities. Its primary goals include:

- **Asset Discovery:** Maintaining comprehensive visibility of all network-connected devices
- **Access Control:** Preventing unauthorized device connections
- **Lifecycle Management:** Managing assets from acquisition through retirement
- **Risk Management:** Reducing attack surface through proper asset control

CHAPTER 4: IMPLEMENTING ENTERPRISE ASSET CONTROLS (CONTROLS...

Implementation Checklist

Technical Prerequisites:

- Network segmentation capabilities
- DHCP server logging enabled
- DNS logging configured
- Switch port security features available
- Endpoint management tools deployed
- Network monitoring tools operational
- Asset management database established

Process Requirements:

- Asset onboarding procedures documented
- Device authorization process established
- Asset retirement workflows defined
- Emergency device procedures documented
- Asset ownership model defined
- Regular audit schedule established
- Incident response procedures for unauthorized devices
- Asset tagging standards implemented
- Inventory reconciliation process defined

Security Requirements:

- Network access control policies established
- Asset security baseline standards documented

- Minimum security requirements by asset type
- Vulnerability scanning coverage requirements
- Asset monitoring requirements defined
- Security exception process documented

Asset Inventory Templates

Core Asset Record Template:
{
"assetId": "unique_identifier",
"assetType": ["Workstation", "Server", "Network", "IoT", "Mobile"],
"manufacturer": "vendor_name",
"model": "model_number",
"serialNumber": "serial_id",
"purchaseDate": "yyyy-mm-dd",
"warrantyExpiration": "yyyy-mm-dd",
"location": {
"building": "location_name",
"floor": "floor_number",
"room": "room_identifier"
},
"network": {
"macAddress": "xx:xx:xx:xx:xx:xx",
"ipAddress": "xxx.xxx.xxx.xxx",
"subnet": "subnet_identifier",
"vlan": "vlan_number"
},

CHAPTER 4: IMPLEMENTING ENTERPRISE ASSET CONTROLS (CONTROLS...

```
"ownership": {
"department": "dept_name",
"primaryContact": "contact_name",
"technicalOwner": "tech_owner"
},
"security": {
"complianceRequirements": ["PCI", "HIPAA", "SOX"],
"securityZone": "zone_classification",
"lastPatchDate": "yyyy-mm-dd",
"lastScanDate": "yyyy-mm-dd"
},
"lifecycle": {
"status": ["Active", "Maintenance", "Retired"],
"criticality": ["High", "Medium", "Low"],
"maintenanceWindow": "schedule_info",
"endOfLife": "yyyy-mm-dd"
}
}
```

CIS CONTROLS IN PRACTICE

Core Asset Record Form

Identification

Asset ID: _____
Asset Type: [Workstation | Server | Network | IoT | Mobile]
Manufacturer: _____
Model: _____
Serial Number: _____
Purchase Date: [/ /]
Warranty Expiration: [/ /]

Location

Building: _____
Floor: _____
Room: _____

Network

MAC Address: __:__:__:__:__:__
IP Address: __.__.__.__
Subnet: _____
VLAN: _____

Ownership

Department: _____
Primary Contact: _____
Technical Owner: _____

Security

Compliance Requirements: [PCI | HIPAA | SOX]
Security Zone: [High | Medium | Low]
Last Patch Date: [/ /]
Last Scan Date: [/ /]

Lifecycle

Status: [Active | Maintenance | Retired]
Criticality: [High | Medium | Low]
Maintenance Window: _____
End of Life: [/ /]

Implementation Steps

Phase 1: Foundation Setup (Weeks 1-4)

1. Network Preparation

- Enable DHCP logging
- Configure switch port security
- Enable 802.1x where applicable
- Set up network monitoring
- Configure DNS logging

2. Tool Deployment

- Install network discovery tools
- Configure asset management database
- Deploy endpoint management agents
- Set up NAC solution
- Configure vulnerability scanners

Phase 2: Initial Discovery (Weeks 5-8)

1. Active Discovery

- Run comprehensive network scans
- Execute port scans
- Perform DNS enumeration
- Conduct wireless network surveys
- Document discovered assets

2. Passive Monitoring

- Enable netflow collection
- Monitor DHCP requests

- Track DNS queries
- Analyze network traffic
- Record discovered assets

Phase 3: Process Implementation (Weeks 9-12)

1. Asset Management

- Document asset workflows
- Establish ownership model
- Define lifecycle processes
- Create authorization procedures
- Set up tagging system

2. Security Controls

- Implement access controls
- Configure alerting rules
- Establish baseline configurations
- Define security exceptions
- Document incident response

Phase 4: Operational Integration (Weeks 13-16)

1. Process Integration

- Connect with change management
- Link to incident management
- Integrate with CMDB

- Align with security operations
- Establish reporting procedures

Tools and Resources

Network Discovery Tools:

- **Nmap for network scanning**
- **Configuration:** sudo nmap -sS -O -v [network_range]
- **Use case:** Initial network discovery
- **Key features:** OS detection, port scanning

- **Wireshark for traffic analysis**
- **Configuration:** Capture filters for asset discovery
- **Use case:** Passive asset detection
- **Key features:** Protocol analysis, traffic inspection

Asset Management Platforms:

- **ServiceNow Asset Management**
- **Key modules:** Hardware Asset Management, Software Asset Management
- **Integration points:** CMDB, Change Management
- **Automation capabilities:** Discovery integration, lifecycle automation

- **BMC Helix Discovery**
- **Features:** Automated discovery, dependency mapping
- **Use cases:** Data center asset management
- **Integration capabilities:** CMDB synchronization

Network Access Control:

- **Cisco ISE**
- **Implementation scope:** Enterprise-wide NAC
- **Key features:** 802.1x, MAC Authentication Bypass
- **Integration capabilities:** Active Directory, MDM

- **ForeScout CounterACT**
- **Use cases:** IoT device control
- **Key features:** Agentless detection, automated response
- **Integration points:** SIEM, vulnerability scanners

Control 2: Inventory and Control of Software Assets-Comprehensive Implementation Guide

Control Overview

Control 2 focuses on actively managing all software on the network to ensure only authorized software is installed and executed. This control is crucial for reducing the attack surface created by unauthorized and potentially malicious software. The primary goals include:

- **Software Discovery:** Maintaining a comprehensive inventory of all installed software
- **Execution Control:** Preventing unauthorized software from running
- **License Management:** Ensuring compliance with software licensing requirements
- **Version Control:** Managing software versions and updates effectively

Implementation Checklist

Technical Prerequisites:

- Software discovery tools deployed
- Application whitelisting capability
- Package management systems configured
- Software distribution platform operational
- License tracking system implemented
- Version monitoring tools deployed
- Software repository established
- Code signing infrastructure ready

Process Requirements:

- Software approval workflow documented
- License management procedures established
- Software retirement process defined
- Emergency software procedures documented
- Software categorization model implemented
- Regular audit schedule defined
- Version control procedures established
- Software request process documented
- Patch management workflow defined

Security Requirements:

- Application control policies established
- Software baseline standards documented
- Minimum security requirements by software type
- Vulnerability management requirements defined
- Software monitoring standards established
- Security exception process documented
- Code signing requirements defined
- Third-party software vetting process

Software Inventory Templates

Core Software Record Template:
{
"softwareId": "unique_identifier",
"softwareName": "application_name",

CHAPTER 4: IMPLEMENTING ENTERPRISE ASSET CONTROLS (CONTROLS...

```
"publisher": "vendor_name",
"version": "version_number",
"releaseDate": "yyyy-mm-dd",
"endOfSupport": "yyyy-mm-dd",
"installationDetails": {
"installPath": "installation_location",
"installDate": "yyyy-mm-dd",
"installedBy": "user_name",
"installationType": ["Standard", "Custom"]
},
"licensing": {
"licenseType": ["Enterprise", "Individual", "Site"],
"licenseKey": "key_identifier",
"expirationDate": "yyyy-mm-dd",
"seats": "number_of_licenses"
},
"security": {
"approvalStatus": ["Approved", "Restricted", "Prohibited"],
"securityClassification": ["Critical", "High", "Medium", "Low"],
"lastPatchDate": "yyyy-mm-dd",
"knownVulnerabilities": "CVE_list"
},
"deployment": {
"deploymentMethod": ["Automated", "Manual"],
"targetSystems": "system_list",
"requiredPermissions": "permission_set",
"dependencies": "dependency_list"
},
"compliance": {
"regulatoryRequirements": ["PCI", "HIPAA", "SOX"],
"complianceStatus": ["Compliant", "Non-compliant"],
```

"lastAuditDate": "yyyy-mm-dd",
"auditFindings": "finding_summary"
}
}

CHAPTER 4: IMPLEMENTING ENTERPRISE ASSET CONTROLS (CONTROLS...

Core Software Record Form

Software Information

Software ID: _____
Software Name: _____
Publisher: _____
Version: _____
Release Date: [/ /]
End of Support: [/ /]

Installation Details

Install Path: _____
Install Date: [/ /]
Installed By: _____
Installation Type: [Standard | Custom]

Licensing

License Type: [Enterprise | Individual | Site]
License Key: _____
Expiration Date: [/ /]
Seats: _____

Security

Approval Status: [Approved | Restricted | Prohibited]
Security Classification: [Critical | High | Medium | Low]
Last Patch Date: [/ /]
Known Vulnerabilities: _____

Deployment

Deployment Method: [Automated | Manual]
Target Systems: _____
Required Permissions: _____
Dependencies: _____

Compliance

Regulatory Requirements: [PCI | HIPAA | SOX]
Compliance Status: [Compliant | Non-compliant]
Last Audit Date: [/ /]
Audit Findings: _____

Implementation Steps

Phase 1: Foundation Setup (Weeks 1-4)

1. Discovery Infrastructure

- Deploy software inventory tools
- Configure application control systems
- Set up software repositories
- Implement license tracking
- Configure monitoring systems

2. Process Development

- Create software approval workflows
- Establish license management procedures
- Define software categorization
- Document baseline configurations
- Develop audit procedures

Phase 2: Initial Discovery (Weeks 5-8)

1. Software Discovery

- Run automated discovery scans
- Conduct manual inventory
- Document installed applications
- Identify unauthorized software
- Map software dependencies

2. License Assessment

- Audit existing licenses
- Document license assignments
- Identify compliance gaps
- Create license inventory
- Establish renewal tracking

Phase 3: Control Implementation (Weeks 9-12)

1. Application Control

- Deploy whitelisting solutions
- Configure blacklisting rules
- Implement execution control
- Set up monitoring alerts
- Test control effectiveness

2. Process Integration

- Connect with change management
- Integrate with asset management
- Link to security operations
- Establish reporting procedures
- Implement automated workflows

Tools and Resources

Software Discovery Tools:

- **Microsoft SCCM**
- **Configuration:** Asset Intelligence settings
- **Use case:** Enterprise software inventory
- **Key features:** Automated discovery, reporting

- **Flexera Software Asset Management**
- **Features:** License optimization, usage tracking
- **Use case:** License compliance management
- **Key capabilities:** Software recognition library

Application Control Tools:

- **Microsoft AppLocker**
- **Implementation scope:** Windows environment
- **Key features:** Rule-based control, group policies
- **Deployment considerations:** Testing requirements

- **Carbon Black**
- **Use cases:** Endpoint protection, application control
- **Key features:** Behavioral analysis, threat prevention
- **Integration capabilities:** SIEM, threat intelligence

License Management Platforms:

- **Snow License Manager**
- **Features:** License optimization, compliance reporting
- **Use case:** Enterprise license management
- **Integration points:** ITSM systems, procurement

- **ServiceNow Software Asset Management**
- **Key modules:** Discovery, License Management
- **Integration capabilities:** CMDB, Purchase Management
- **Automation features:** License reconciliation

Control 3: Data Protection- Comprehensive Implementation Guide

Control Overview

Control 3 focuses on developing and implementing processes and technical controls to identify, classify, securely handle, retain, and dispose of data. This control ensures organizations protect sensitive information throughout its lifecycle. Primary goals include:

- **Data Discovery:** Identifying and mapping all sensitive data locations
- **Classification:** Implementing effective data classification

schemes
- **Access Control:** Ensuring appropriate data access restrictions
- **Encryption:** Protecting data through proper encryption
- **Data Lifecycle:** Managing data from creation through disposal

Implementation Checklist

Technical Prerequisites:

- Data discovery tools deployed
- Data Loss Prevention (DLP) systems
- Encryption solutions implemented
- Access control systems configured
- Backup systems operational
- Data classification tools ready
- Monitoring systems active
- Secure disposal tools available

Process Requirements:

- Data classification schema defined
- Data handling procedures documented
- Retention policies established
- Disposal procedures documented
- Access review process defined
- Incident response procedures ready
- Data inventory process established

- Regular audit schedule defined
- Data privacy requirements documented

Security Requirements:

- Encryption standards defined
- Access control policies established
- Data transfer controls implemented
- Backup requirements documented
- Monitoring standards established
- Incident handling procedures ready
- Privacy controls implemented
- Security exception process defined

Data Protection Templates

Data Classification Template:
```
{
"dataIdentifier": "unique_identifier",
"classificationType": ["Public", "Internal", "Confidential", "Restricted"],
"dataAttributes": {
"description": "data_description",
"format": ["Structured", "Unstructured"],
"location": ["Database", "File Share", "Cloud"],
"volume": "data_size"
},
```

```
"security": {
"encryptionRequired": ["AtRest", "InTransit", "Both"],
"accessControls": {
"readAccess": "group_list",
"writeAccess": "group_list",
"adminAccess": "group_list"
},
"retentionPeriod": "time_period",
"disposalMethod": ["Secure Delete", "Destruction", "Anonymization"]
},
"compliance": {
"regulations": ["GDPR", "HIPAA", "PCI"],
"auditRequirements": "audit_frequency",
"privacyImpact": ["High", "Medium", "Low"]
},
"handling": {
"storageMethods": ["Approved_Locations"],
"transferMethods": ["Approved_Methods"],
"processingRequirements": "processing_rules"
},
"incident": {
"notificationRequirements": "notification_rules",
"responseProc": "response_procedure_ref",
"escalationPath": "escalation_contacts"
}
}
```

CHAPTER 4: IMPLEMENTING ENTERPRISE ASSET CONTROLS (CONTROLS...

Data Classification Form

Data Identifier

Data Identifier: _____
Classification Type: [Public | Internal | Confidential | Restricted]

Data Attributes

Description: _____
Format: [Structured | Unstructured]
Location: [Database | File Share | Cloud]
Volume: _____

Security

Encryption Required: [AtRest | InTransit | Both]
Read Access: _____
Write Access: _____
Admin Access: _____
Retention Period: _____
Disposal Method: [Secure Delete | Destruction | Anonymization]

Compliance

Regulations: [GDPR | HIPAA | PCI]
Audit Requirements: _____
Privacy Impact: [High | Medium | Low]

Handling

Storage Methods: _____
Transfer Methods: _____
Processing Requirements: _____

Incident Management

Notification Requirements: _____
Response Procedure: _____
Escalation Path: _____

Implementation Steps

Phase 1: Foundation Setup (Weeks 1-6)

1. Data Discovery Setup

- Deploy discovery tools
- Configure scanning parameters
- Establish baseline inventory
- Map data flows
- Document data repositories

2. Classification Implementation

- Define classification levels
- Implement labeling systems
- Configure automated classification
- Train users on classification
- Validate classification accuracy

Phase 2: Protection Implementation (Weeks 7-12)

1. Access Control

- Configure access policies
- Implement role-based access
- Set up authentication controls
- Deploy monitoring tools
- Test access restrictions

2. Encryption Deployment

- Configure encryption tools
- Implement key management
- Set up secure transfer methods
- Test encryption effectiveness
- Document recovery procedures

Phase 3: Monitoring and Management (Weeks 13-18)

1. DLP Implementation

- Deploy DLP solutions
- Configure monitoring rules
- Establish alert procedures
- Test detection capabilities
- Document response procedures

2. Lifecycle Management

- Implement retention policies
- Configure disposal procedures
- Set up audit logging
- Establish review processes
- Test recovery procedures

Tools and Resources

Data Discovery Tools:

- **Varonis Data Classification Engine**
- **Features:** Automated classification, risk analysis
- **Use case:** Unstructured data discovery
- **Key capabilities:** Pattern matching, content analysis

- **Spirion Sensitive Data Manager**
- **Implementation scope:** Enterprise-wide discovery
- **Key features:** Automated scanning, remediation
- **Integration points:** DLP, SIEM systems

Encryption Solutions:

- **Microsoft BitLocker**
- **Use case:** Endpoint encryption
- **Key features:** TPM integration, key management
- **Deployment considerations:** Recovery planning

- **Thales CipherTrust**
- **Features:** Enterprise encryption management
- **Use case:** Database and file encryption
- **Integration capabilities:** Key management, SIEM

DLP Platforms:

- **Symantec DLP**
- **Key modules:** Network, Endpoint, Cloud
- **Integration points:** CASB, SIEM
- **Detection capabilities:** Pattern matching, ML-based

- **Microsoft Information Protection**
- **Features:** Classification, protection, monitoring
- **Use case:** Microsoft ecosystem protection
- **Automation capabilities:** Policy enforcement

Control 4: Secure Configuration of Enterprise Assets and Software- Comprehensive Implementation Guide

Control Overview

Control 4 focuses on establishing and maintaining the secure configuration of enterprise assets and software. This control ensures organizations implement and actively manage the security configuration of their IT infrastructure using a rigorous configuration management and change control process. Primary goals include:

- **Configuration Management:** Maintaining secure configurations across all assets
- **Baseline Development:** Creating and maintaining security baselines
- **Change Control:** Managing configuration changes securely
- **Compliance Monitoring:** Ensuring continuous compliance with baselines

Implementation Checklist

Technical Prerequisites:

- Configuration management database (CMDB)

CHAPTER 4: IMPLEMENTING ENTERPRISE ASSET CONTROLS (CONTROLS...

- Security configuration assessment tools
- Automated remediation capabilities
- Change management system
- Version control system
- Backup solutions
- Monitoring tools
- Testing environment

Process Requirements:

- Baseline configuration standards
- Change control procedures
- Configuration review process
- Exception handling workflow
- Emergency change procedures
- Testing protocols defined
- Rollback procedures
- Audit schedule established
- Documentation requirements

Security Requirements:

- Hardening standards documented
- Configuration validation process
- Drift detection capabilities
- Compliance checking automated
- Security testing procedures
- Exception management process
- Incident response procedures

- Access control requirements

Configuration Management Templates

Secure Configuration Template:
```
{
"configurationId": "unique_identifier",
"assetType": ["Server", "Workstation", "Network", "Application"],
"baselineDetails": {
"baselineVersion": "version_number",
"releaseDate": "yyyy-mm-dd",
"approvedBy": "approver_name",
"applicability": "asset_scope"
},
"securitySettings": {
"accountPolicies": {
"passwordComplexity": "policy_details",
"accountLockout": "lockout_settings",
"privilegedAccess": "privilege_rules"
},
"systemServices": {
"requiredServices": "service_list",
"disabledServices": "service_list",
"serviceConfig": "config_details"
},
"networkSecurity": {
"firewallRules": "rule_set",
```

CHAPTER 4: IMPLEMENTING ENTERPRISE ASSET CONTROLS (CONTROLS...

```
"portConfiguration": "port_settings",
"protocolSettings": "protocol_rules"
}
},
"compliance": {
"standards": ["CIS", "NIST", "DISA"],
"exceptions": "exception_list",
"compensatingControls": "control_details"
},
"changeControl": {
"lastModified": "yyyy-mm-dd",
"modifiedBy": "user_name",
"changeTicket": "ticket_reference",
"approvalChain": "approver_list"
},
"validation": {
"lastChecked": "yyyy-mm-dd",
"complianceStatus": ["Compliant", "Non-compliant"],
"deviations": "deviation_list",
"remediationPlan": "remediation_details"
}
}
```

CIS CONTROLS IN PRACTICE

Secure Configuration Form

Configuration Information

Configuration ID: _____
Asset Type: [Server | Workstation | Network | Application]

Baseline Details

Baseline Version: _____
Release Date: [/ /]
Approved By: _____
Applicability: _____

Security Settings - Account Policies

Password Complexity: _____
Account Lockout: _____
Privileged Access: _____

Security Settings - System Services

Required Services: _____
Disabled Services: _____
Service Configuration: _____

Security Settings - Network Security

Firewall Rules: _____
Port Configuration: _____
Protocol Settings: _____

Compliance

Standards: [CIS | NIST | DISA]
Exceptions: _____
Compensating Controls: _____

Change Control

Last Modified: [/ /]
Modified By: _____
Change Ticket: _____
Approval Chain: _____

Validation

Last Checked: [/ /]
Compliance Status: [Compliant | Non-compliant]
Deviations: _____
Remediation Plan: _____

Implementation Steps

Phase 1: Baseline Development (Weeks 1-6)

1. Standard Development

- Research security standards
- Define organizational requirements
- Create baseline configurations
- Document security settings
- Establish validation criteria

2. Tool Implementation

- Deploy configuration tools
- Set up monitoring systems
- Configure assessment tools
- Implement backup solutions
- Test automation capabilities

Phase 2: Initial Implementation (Weeks 7-12)

1. Configuration Deployment

- Apply baseline configurations
- Validate security settings
- Document exceptions
- Test functionality
- Monitor for issues

2. Process Integration

- Implement change control
- Configure automation
- Establish monitoring
- Set up reporting
- Train support staff

Phase 3: Operational Integration (Weeks 13-18)

1. Compliance Management

- Configure compliance checks
- Establish audit procedures
- Implement drift detection
- Set up reporting
- Define remediation processes

2. Continuous Improvement

- Monitor effectiveness
- Gather feedback
- Refine processes
- Update documentation
- Enhance automation

Tools and Resources

Configuration Management Tools:

- **Microsoft SCCM**
- **Features:** Configuration deployment, compliance monitoring
- **Use case:** Windows environment management
- **Key capabilities:** Automated deployment, reporting

- **Ansible Automation Platform**
- **Implementation scope:** Cross-platform configuration
- **Key features:** Automation, compliance as code
- **Integration capabilities:** Version control, CI/CD

Security Configuration Assessment:

- **Tenable Nessus**
- **Features:** Configuration auditing, compliance checking
- **Use case:** Security posture assessment
- **Key capabilities:** Custom audit policies, reporting

- **CIS-CAT Pro**
- **Implementation scope:** CIS Benchmark assessment
- **Key features:** Automated assessment, remediation
- **Integration points:** SIEM, vulnerability management

Change Management Platforms:

- **ServiceNow Change Management**
- **Features:** Workflow automation, approval tracking
- **Use case:** Enterprise change control
- **Integration capabilities:** CMDB, ITSM

- **BMC Remedy**
- **Key modules:** Change Management, Asset Management
- **Integration points:** CMDB, Service Management
- **Automation features:** Workflow orchestration

Chapter 5: Implementing Account and Access Management Controls (Controls 5-6)

Control 5: Account Management- Comprehensive Implementation Guide

Control Overview

Control 5 focuses on creating, managing, and monitoring all enterprise accounts through their complete lifecycle. This control ensures organizations maintain proper control over resource access through systematic account management. Primary goals include:

- **Account Lifecycle:** Managing accounts from creation through deactivation
- **Privilege Management:** Controlling privileged account access
- **Authentication:** Implementing strong authentication mechanisms
- **Account Monitoring:** Detecting and responding to suspicious activity

Implementation Checklist

Technical Prerequisites:

- Identity Management System (IdM)
- Directory Services infrastructure
- Privileged Access Management (PAM)
- Multi-factor Authentication (MFA)
- Account monitoring tools
- Password management system
- Audit logging system
- Automation platform

Process Requirements:

- Account request procedures
- Approval workflows defined
- Access review process
- Privilege escalation process
- Deprovisioning procedures
- Emergency access protocol
- Audit schedule established
- Password policy documented
- Account naming standards

Security Requirements:

- Authentication standards

CHAPTER 5: IMPLEMENTING ACCOUNT AND ACCESS MANAGEMENT...

- Password complexity rules
- Account lockout policies
- Session timeout settings
- Access review requirements
- Monitoring standards
- Incident response procedures
- Compliance requirements

Account Management Templates

Account Lifecycle Template:
```
{
"accountId": "unique_identifier",
"accountType": ["Standard", "Privileged", "Service", "Emergency"],
  "userDetails": {
"employeeId": "employee_number",
"department": "department_name",
"role": "job_title",
"manager": "manager_name"
},
"accessProfile": {
"baseAccess": "profile_name",
"additionalAccess": "access_list",
"privileges": "privilege_level",
"restrictions": "restriction_list"
},
"authentication": {
```

```
"method": ["Password", "MFA", "Certificate"],
"lastPasswordChange": "yyyy-mm-dd",
"mfaStatus": "status_details",
"passwordExpiry": "yyyy-mm-dd"
},
"lifecycle": {
"creationDate": "yyyy-mm-dd",
"lastReview": "yyyy-mm-dd",
"expirationDate": "yyyy-mm-dd",
"status": ["Active", "Suspended", "Terminated"]
},
"compliance": {
"lastAudit": "yyyy-mm-dd",
"findings": "audit_results",
"exceptions": "exception_list",
"certifications": "cert_requirements"
},
"activity": {
"lastLogin": "yyyy-mm-dd",
"failedAttempts": "number",
"unusualActivity": "activity_list",
"locationAccess": "location_list"
}
}
```

CHAPTER 5: IMPLEMENTING ACCOUNT AND ACCESS MANAGEMENT...

Account Lifecycle Form

Account Information

Account ID: _____
Account Type: [Standard | Privileged | Service | Emergency]

User Details

Employee ID: _____
Department: _____
Role: _____
Manager: _____

Access Profile

Base Access: _____
Additional Access: _____
Privileges: _____
Restrictions: _____

Authentication

Method: [Password | MFA | Certificate]
Last Password Change: [/ /]
MFA Status: _____
Password Expiry: [/ /]

Lifecycle

Creation Date: [/ /]
Last Review: [/ /]
Expiration Date: [/ /]
Status: [Active | Suspended | Terminated]

Compliance

Last Audit: [/ /]
Findings: _____
Exceptions: _____
Certifications: _____

Activity

Last Login: [/ /]
Failed Attempts: _____
Unusual Activity: _____
Location Access: _____

Implementation Steps

Phase 1: Foundation Setup (Weeks 1-6)

1. Infrastructure Preparation

- Deploy identity management system
- Configure directory services
- Implement PAM solution
- Set up MFA infrastructure
- Configure monitoring tools

2. Policy Development

- Create account policies
- Define password standards
- Establish review procedures
- Document workflows
- Set up automation

Phase 2: Account Implementation (Weeks 7-12)

1. Account Structure

- Implement naming convention
- Configure account types
- Set up access profiles
- Establish hierarchies
- Define permissions

2. Authentication Setup

- Deploy password management
- Configure MFA
- Implement SSO
- Set up session management
- Test authentication flows

Phase 3: Monitoring and Control (Weeks 13-18)

1. Monitoring Implementation

- Configure audit logging
- Set up alerts
- Implement reporting
- Establish reviews
- Test detection capabilities

2. Process Integration

- Connect with HR systems
- Integrate change management
- Implement automation
- Set up workflows
- Document procedures

Tools and Resources

Identity Management Tools:

- **Microsoft Azure AD**
- **Features:** Cloud identity management, MFA
- **Use case:** Enterprise identity management
- **Key capabilities:** SSO, conditional access

- **Okta Identity Cloud**
- **Implementation scope:** Enterprise IAM
- **Key features:** Lifecycle management, automation
- **Integration capabilities:** HR systems, applications

Privileged Access Management:

- **CyberArk Privileged Access Security**
- **Features:** Privileged account management, monitoring
- **Use case:** Privileged access control
- **Key capabilities:** Password vault, session recording

- **BeyondTrust Privileged Access Management**
- **Implementation scope:** Privileged account control
- **Key features:** Just-in-time access, monitoring
- **Integration points:** SIEM, identity management

Account Monitoring Tools:

- **SailPoint IdentityIQ**
- **Features:** Access certification, compliance
- **Use case:** Identity governance
- **Integration capabilities:** HR, IT systems

- **RSA SecurID Suite**
- **Key modules:** Authentication, lifecycle management
- **Integration points:** Directory services, applications
- **Automation features:** Access provisioning

Control 6: Access Control Management- Comprehensive Implementation Guide

Control Overview

Control 6 focuses on creating, managing, and monitoring access control rules that enforce authenticated access to enterprise assets and software. This control ensures that organizations implement the principle of least privilege and maintain the separation of duties. Primary goals include:

- **Access Governance:** Managing access rights and permissions
- **Authorization Control:** Implementing role-based access control

- **Permission Management:** Maintaining granular access controls
- **Access Monitoring:** Detecting unauthorized access attempts

Implementation Checklist

Technical Prerequisites:

- Access Control System (ACS)
- Role-based Access Control (RBAC)
- Attribute-based Access Control (ABAC)
- Authorization framework
- Policy enforcement points
- Access monitoring tools
- Workflow automation
- Audit logging system

Process Requirements:

- Access request procedures
- Role definition process
- Permission review workflow
- Separation of duties matrix
- Emergency access procedures
- Change control process
- Review schedule defined
- Exception handling process
- Documentation standards

Security Requirements:

- Authorization policies
- Access control rules
- Permission boundaries
- Monitoring requirements
- Alert thresholds
- Incident response procedures
- Compliance requirements
- Risk assessment criteria

Access Control Templates

Access Policy Template:
```
{
"policyId": "unique_identifier",
"policyType": ["Role", "Resource", "Application"],
"accessRules": {
"permissions": "permission_set",
"conditions": "access_conditions",
"restrictions": "restriction_list",
"exceptions": "exception_cases"
},
"roleDefinition": {
"roleName": "role_identifier",
"description": "role_description",
"responsibilities": "duty_list",
"restrictions": "limitation_list"
```

},
"enforcement": {
"mechanism": ["RBAC", "ABAC", "Hybrid"],
"technicalControls": "control_list",
"compensatingControls": "control_details",
"validationRules": "validation_criteria"
},
"compliance": {
"requirements": ["SOX", "HIPAA", "PCI"],
"reviewCycle": "review_frequency",
"attestationNeeded": "attestation_requirements",
"documentation": "required_documents"
},
"monitoring": {
"alertTriggers": "alert_conditions",
"reviewProcess": "review_procedures",
"auditTrail": "audit_requirements",
"metrics": "measurement_criteria"
}
}

CHAPTER 5: IMPLEMENTING ACCOUNT AND ACCESS MANAGEMENT...

Access Policy Form

Policy Information

Policy ID: _____
Policy Type: [Role | Resource | Application]

Access Rules

Permissions: _____
Conditions: _____
Restrictions: _____
Exceptions: _____

Role Definition

Role Name: _____
Description: _____
Responsibilities: _____
Restrictions: _____

Enforcement

Mechanism: [RBAC | ABAC | Hybrid]
Technical Controls: _____
Compensating Controls: _____
Validation Rules: _____

Compliance

Requirements: [SOX | HIPAA | PCI]
Review Cycle: _____
Attestation Needed: _____
Documentation: _____

Monitoring

Alert Triggers: _____
Review Process: _____
Audit Trail: _____
Metrics: _____

Implementation Steps

Phase 1: Foundation Setup (Weeks 1-6)

1. Policy Development

- Define access policies
- Create role matrices
- Establish workflows
- Document procedures
- Design review processes

2. Infrastructure Setup

- Deploy access control system
- Configure RBAC framework
- Implement monitoring
- Set up automation
- Configure logging

Phase 2: Role Implementation (Weeks 7-12)

1. Role Definition

- Create role hierarchy
- Define permissions
- Establish boundaries
- Configure restrictions
- Test access rules

2. Access Implementation

- Deploy access policies
- Configure enforcement
- Implement workflows
- Set up reviews
- Test controls

Phase 3: Monitoring Setup (Weeks 13-18)

1. Control Monitoring

- Configure alerts
- Implement reporting
- Establish metrics
- Set up dashboards
- Test detection

2. Process Integration

- Connect systems
- Implement automation
- Configure workflows
- Document procedures
- Train staff

Tools and Resources

Access Control Systems:

- **SailPoint IdentityNow**
- **Features:** Access governance, certification
- **Use case:** Enterprise access management
- **Key capabilities:** Role mining, automation

- **ForgeRock Identity Platform**
- **Implementation scope:** Access management
- **Key features:** Fine-grained authorization
- **Integration capabilities:** APIs, applications

Authorization Tools:

- **PlainID Authorization Platform**
- **Features:** Policy management, enforcement
- **Use case:** Dynamic authorization
- **Key capabilities:** Real-time decisions

- **Axiomatics Policy Server**
- **Implementation scope:** ABAC implementation
- **Key features:** Dynamic authorization
- **Integration points:** Applications, services

Monitoring Solutions:

- **Varonis Data Security Platform**
- **Features:** Access monitoring, analytics
- **Use case:** Data access control
- **Integration capabilities:** SIEM, DLP

- **One Identity Manager**
- **Key modules:** Access governance, compliance
- **Integration points:** Directory services
- **Automation features:** Policy enforcement

Chapter 6: Implementing Continuous Monitoring and Defense Controls (Controls 7-14)

Control 7: Continuous Vulnerability Management- Comprehensive Implementation Guide

Control Overview

Control 7 focuses on establishing and maintaining a continuous vulnerability management program to identify, evaluate, report on, and remediate security vulnerabilities. This control ensures organizations proactively identify and address security weaknesses before they can be exploited. Primary goals include:

- **Vulnerability Discovery:** Continuously identifying security vulnerabilities
- **Risk Assessment:** Evaluating and prioritizing vulnerabilities
- **Remediation Management:** Addressing vulnerabilities systematically

CHAPTER 6: IMPLEMENTING CONTINUOUS MONITORING AND DEFENSE...

- **Compliance Monitoring:** Ensuring ongoing security compliance

Implementation Checklist

Technical Prerequisites:

- Vulnerability scanning tools
- Asset management system
- Patch management platform
- Risk assessment framework
- Remediation tracking system
- Configuration management
- Testing environment
- Monitoring infrastructure

Process Requirements:

- Scanning procedures
- Assessment workflows
- Remediation processes
- Exception handling
- Emergency patching
- Change control
- Testing protocols
- Review schedules
- Documentation standards

Security Requirements:

- Scanning policies
- Risk scoring criteria
- Remediation SLAs
- Monitoring standards
- Alert thresholds
- Testing requirements
- Compliance mapping
- Reporting standards

Vulnerability Management Templates

Vulnerability Assessment Template:
```
{
"vulnerabilityId": "unique_identifier",
"discoveryDetails": {
"dateIdentified": "yyyy-mm-dd",
"source": ["Scan", "Penetration Test", "Threat Intel"],
"affectedAssets": "asset_list",
"scanReference": "scan_identifier"
},
"vulnerabilityInfo": {
"cveId": "CVE-identifier",
"description": "vulnerability_description",
"category": "vulnerability_type",
"exploitability": ["High", "Medium", "Low"]
},
```

```
"riskAssessment": {
"severity": ["Critical", "High", "Medium", "Low"],
"impactScore": "cvss_score",
"businessImpact": "impact_assessment",
"exploitStatus": "exploit_availability"
},
"remediation": {
"priority": "priority_level",
"solution": "remediation_steps",
"patchAvailable": "patch_details",
"workaround": "temporary_solution",
"timeline": "completion_target"
},
"tracking": {
"status": ["Open", "In Progress", "Resolved"],
"assignedTo": "owner_name",
"nextReview": "yyyy-mm-dd",
"progress": "completion_percentage"
},
"compliance": {
"requirements": ["PCI", "HIPAA", "SOX"],
"exceptions": "exception_details",
"compensatingControls": "control_list",
"documentation": "required_docs"
}
}
```

CIS CONTROLS IN PRACTICE

Vulnerability Assessment Form

Vulnerability Information

Vulnerability ID: _____

Discovery Details

Date Identified: [/ /]
Source: [Scan | Penetration Test | Threat Intel]
Affected Assets: _____
Scan Reference: _____

Vulnerability Info

CVE ID: _____
Description: _____
Category: _____
Exploitability: [High | Medium | Low]

Risk Assessment

Severity: [Critical | High | Medium | Low]
Impact Score: _____
Business Impact: _____
Exploit Status: _____

Remediation

Priority: _____
Solution: _____
Patch Available: _____
Workaround: _____
Timeline: [/ /]

Tracking

Status: [Open | In Progress | Resolved]
Assigned To: _____
Next Review: [/ /]
Progress: _____

Compliance

Requirements: [PCI | HIPAA | SOX]
Exceptions: _____
Compensating Controls: _____
Documentation: _____

Implementation Steps

Phase 1: Foundation Setup (Weeks 1-6)

1. Infrastructure Preparation

- Deploy scanning tools
- Configure asset inventory
- Set up management console
- Implement automation
- Configure reporting

2. Process Development

- Define scanning policies
- Create workflows
- Establish procedures
- Document standards
- Set up training

Phase 2: Scanning Implementation (Weeks 7-12)

1. Scanning Setup

- Configure scan profiles
- Define schedules
- Set up credentials
- Test scanning
- Validate results

2. **Assessment Integration**

- Implement scoring
- Configure prioritization
- Set up tracking
- Establish metrics
- Test reporting

Phase 3: Remediation Management (Weeks 13-18)

1. **Remediation Process**

- Define workflows
- Set up tracking
- Implement automation
- Configure notifications
- Test procedures

2. **Program Integration**

- Connect systems
- Implement dashboards
- Configure alerts
- Establish reviews
- Document processes

Tools and Resources

Vulnerability Scanning Tools:

- **Tenable.io**
- **Features:** Cloud-based scanning, analytics
- **Use case:** Enterprise vulnerability management
- **Key capabilities:** Continuous assessment, automation

- **Qualys Vulnerability Management**
- **Implementation scope:** Network and cloud scanning
- **Key features:** Asset discovery, threat prioritization
- **Integration capabilities:** CMDB, SIEM

Patch Management Tools:

- **Microsoft WSUS**
- **Features:** Windows update management
- **Use case:** Microsoft environment patching
- **Key capabilities:** Automated deployment, reporting

- **Ivanti Security Controls**
- **Implementation scope:** Cross-platform patching
- **Key features:** Patch automation, compliance
- **Integration points:** Asset management, SIEM

Risk Assessment Platforms:

- **Rapid7 InsightVM**
- **Features:** Risk-based vulnerability management
- **Use case:** Prioritized remediation
- **Integration capabilities:** DevOps, cloud

- **Brinqa Risk Platform**
- **Key modules:** Risk analytics, automation
- **Integration points:** Security tools, IT systems
- **Automation features:** Risk prioritization

Control 8: Audit Log Management- Comprehensive Implementation Guide

Control Overview

Control 8 collects, alerts, and manages audit logs of security-relevant events across enterprise assets and software. This control ensures organizations maintain comprehensive visibility into their security posture through effective log collection and analysis. Primary goals include:

- **Log Collection:** Gathering security-relevant events
- **Log Analysis:** Detecting security incidents and anomalies

- **Log Protection:** Securing audit log data
- **Incident Detection:** Identifying security events promptly

Implementation Checklist

Technical Prerequisites:

- Security Information and Event Management (SIEM)
- Log collection infrastructure
- Log storage solutions
- Analysis platforms
- Alert management system
- Archive solutions
- Monitoring tools
- Automation platform

Process Requirements:

- Log collection policies
- Retention schedules
- Analysis procedures
- Alert workflows
- Review processes
- Storage management
- Archive procedures
- Incident response integration
- Documentation standards

Security Requirements:

- Log integrity controls
- Access restrictions
- Encryption requirements
- Monitoring standards
- Alert thresholds
- Compliance requirements
- Retention policies
- Security controls

Audit Log Management Templates

Log Management Configuration Template:
```
{
"logSourceId": "unique_identifier",
"sourceDetails": {
"sourceType": ["System", "Application", "Security", "Network"],
"location": "source_location",
"format": "log_format",
"priority": ["High", "Medium", "Low"]
},
"collectionConfig": {
"method": ["Agent", "Syslog", "API"],
"frequency": "collection_interval",
"filters": "filter_rules",
"transformation": "parsing_rules"
},
```

CHAPTER 6: IMPLEMENTING CONTINUOUS MONITORING AND DEFENSE...

```
"retention": {
"onlinePeriod": "time_period",
"archivePeriod": "time_period",
"storageLocation": "storage_details",
"compressionMethod": "compression_type"
},
"security": {
"encryption": ["AtRest", "InTransit"],
"accessControl": "access_rules",
"integrityChecks": "check_methods",
"monitoring": "monitoring_rules"
},
"analysis": {
"correlationRules": "rule_set",
"alertThresholds": "threshold_values",
"automaticActions": "action_list",
"reportingRequirements": "report_specs"
},
"compliance": {
"requirements": ["SOX", "PCI", "HIPAA"],
"retentionPeriods": "retention_rules",
"auditTrail": "audit_requirements",
"documentation": "required_docs"
}
}
```

CIS CONTROLS IN PRACTICE

Log Management Configuration Form

Log Source Information

Log Source ID: _____
Source Type: [System | Application | Security | Network]
Location: _____
Format: _____
Priority: [High | Medium | Low]

Collection Configuration

Method: [Agent | Syslog | API]
Frequency: _____
Filters: _____
Transformation: _____

Retention

Online Period: _____
Archive Period: _____
Storage Location: _____
Compression Method: _____

Security

Encryption: [AtRest | InTransit]
Access Control: _____
Integrity Checks: _____
Monitoring: _____

Analysis

Correlation Rules: _____
Alert Thresholds: _____
Automatic Actions: _____
Reporting Requirements: _____

Compliance

Requirements: [SOX | PCI | HIPAA]
Retention Periods: _____
Audit Trail: _____
Documentation: _____

Implementation Steps

Phase 1: Foundation Setup (Weeks 1-6)

1. Infrastructure Preparation

- Deploy SIEM solution
- Configure collectors
- Set up storage
- Implement encryption
- Configure retention

2. Policy Development

- Define collection requirements
- Create retention policies
- Establish procedures
- Document standards
- Set up workflows

Phase 2: Collection Implementation (Weeks 7-12)

1. Source Integration

- Configure log sources
- Implement parsing
- Set up normalization
- Test collection
- Validate integrity

2. Analysis Setup

- Configure correlation
- Implement alerts
- Set up dashboards
- Establish reporting
- Test detection

Phase 3: Operational Integration (Weeks 13-18)

1. Process Integration

- Connect with incident response
- Implement workflows
- Configure automation
- Set up archiving
- Test procedures

2. Program Optimization

- Fine-tune collection
- Optimize storage
- Enhance detection
- Improve reporting
- Document procedures

Tools and Resources

SIEM Solutions:

- **Splunk Enterprise Security**
- **Features:** Real-time monitoring, analytics
- **Use case:** Enterprise log management
- **Key capabilities:** Advanced correlation, automation

- **IBM QRadar**
- **Implementation scope:** Enterprise SIEM
- **Key features:** Threat detection, compliance
- **Integration capabilities:** Threat intelligence, SOAR

Log Collection Tools:

- **Elastic Stack**
- **Features:** Log collection, analysis
- **Use case:** Centralized logging
- **Key capabilities:** Search, visualization

- **Graylog**
- **Implementation scope:** Log management
- **Key features:** Collection, correlation
- **Integration points:** SIEM, storage

Analysis Platforms:

- **Exabeam Security Analytics**
- **Features:** UEBA, threat detection
- **Use case:** Advanced analytics
- **Integration capabilities:** SIEM, SOAR

- **LogRhythm**
- **Key modules:** Collection, analytics
- **Integration points:** Security tools
- **Automation features:** Response automation

Control 9: Email and Web Browser Protections-Comprehensive Implementation Guide

Control Overview

Control 9 implements security controls for email systems and web browsers to protect against phishing, malware, and other web-based threats. This control ensures organizations maintain robust defenses against common attack vectors. Primary goals include:

- **Email Security:** Protecting against phishing and email-based threats
- **Browser Security:** Securing web browsing activities

- **Content Filtering:** Controlling access to malicious content
- **User Protection:** Safeguarding users from common attacks

Implementation Checklist

Technical Prerequisites:

- Email security gateway
- Web filtering solution
- DNS filtering system
- Anti-phishing tools
- Browser management platform
- SSL inspection capability
- Sandboxing environment
- Monitoring infrastructure

Process Requirements:

- Email filtering policies
- Web access policies
- Update procedures
- Exception handling
- Incident response
- User training
- Testing protocols
- Review schedules
- Documentation standards

Security Requirements:

- Filtering rules
- Authentication policies
- Encryption standards
- Monitoring requirements
- Alert thresholds
- Incident procedures
- Compliance mapping
- Testing criteria

Protection Configuration Templates

Email Security Template:
```
{
"policyId": "unique_identifier",
"emailProtection": {
"filteringRules": {
"spam": "filter_criteria",
"malware": "detection_rules",
"phishing": "identification_patterns",
"attachments": "allowed_types"
},
"authentication": {
"spf": "spf_settings",
"dkim": "dkim_config",
"dmarc": "dmarc_policy"
},
```

CHAPTER 6: IMPLEMENTING CONTINUOUS MONITORING AND DEFENSE...

```
"encryption": {
"type": ["TLS", "S/MIME", "PGP"],
"requirements": "encryption_rules",
"certificates": "cert_management"
}
},
"browserSecurity": {
"configuration": {
"allowedPlugins": "plugin_list",
"blockedExtensions": "extension_list",
"securitySettings": "security_config",
"updatePolicy": "update_rules"
},
"contentFiltering": {
"categories": "blocked_categories",
"exceptions": "allowed_sites",
"downloadPolicy": "download_rules",
"sslInspection": "inspection_config"
}
},
"monitoring": {
"alertTriggers": "alert_conditions",
"loggingRequirements": "log_config",
"reportingNeeds": "report_specs",
"reviewSchedule": "review_frequency"
},
"compliance": {
"requirements": ["PCI", "HIPAA", "SOX"],
"documentation": "required_docs",
"auditTrail": "audit_requirements",
"exceptions": "exception_list"
```

}
}

CHAPTER 6: IMPLEMENTING CONTINUOUS MONITORING AND DEFENSE...

Email Security Configuration Form

Policy Information

Policy ID: _____

Email Protection

Spam Filtering Rules: _____
Malware Detection Rules: _____
Phishing Identification Patterns: _____
Allowed Attachments: _____

Authentication

SPF Settings: _____
DKIM Configuration: _____
DMARC Policy: _____

Encryption

Type: [TLS | S/MIME | PGP]
Requirements: _____
Certificates: _____

Browser Security

Allowed Plugins: _____
Blocked Extensions: _____
Security Settings: _____
Update Policy: _____

Content Filtering

Blocked Categories: _____
Exceptions (Allowed Sites): _____
Download Policy: _____
SSL Inspection: _____

Monitoring

Alert Triggers: _____
Logging Requirements: _____
Reporting Needs: _____
Review Schedule: _____

Compliance

Requirements: [PCI | HIPAA | SOX]
Documentation: _____
Audit Trail: _____
Exceptions: _____

Implementation Steps

Phase 1: Foundation Setup (Weeks 1-6)

1. Email Security Implementation

- Deploy security gateway
- Configure filtering
- Implement authentication
- Set up encryption
- Configure monitoring

2. Browser Security Setup

- Deploy management platform
- Configure policies
- Implement filtering
- Set up updates
- Test controls

Phase 2: Protection Implementation (Weeks 7-12)

1. Content Filtering

- Configure categories
- Set up rules
- Implement exceptions
- Test effectiveness
- Document policies

2. User Protection

- Deploy anti-phishing
- Implement sandboxing
- Configure alerts
- Set up training
- Test awareness

Phase 3: Monitoring Integration (Weeks 13-18)

1. Operational Integration

- Connect monitoring
- Implement reporting
- Configure automation
- Set up reviews
- Test procedures

2. Program Optimization

- Fine-tune filters
- Enhance detection
- Improve response
- Update documentation
- Validate effectiveness

Tools and Resources

Email Security Solutions:

- **Proofpoint Email Protection**
- **Features:** Advanced threat defense, email encryption
- **Use case:** Enterprise email security
- **Key capabilities:** AI-powered detection, sandboxing

- **Cisco Email Security**
- **Implementation scope:** Email protection
- **Key features:** Anti-spam, anti-malware
- **Integration capabilities:** Security ecosystem

Web Security Tools:

- **Zscaler Internet Access**
- **Features:** Cloud security, SSL inspection
- **Use case:** Web protection
- **Key capabilities:** Zero trust, cloud sandboxing

- **Cisco Umbrella**
- **Implementation scope:** DNS security
- **Key features:** Web filtering, threat intelligence
- **Integration points:** Security infrastructure

Browser Management:

- **Microsoft Intune**
- **Features:** Browser policy management
- **Use case:** Enterprise browser control
- **Integration capabilities:** Endpoint management

- **Chrome Enterprise**
- **Key modules:** Policy management, security
- **Integration points:** MDM solutions
- **Automation features:** Policy deployment

Control 10: Malware Defenses - Comprehensive Implementation Guide

Control Overview

Control 10 focuses on preventing and detecting malware installation, propagation, and execution across enterprise assets. This control ensures organizations maintain comprehensive protection against various forms of malicious software. Primary goals include:

- **Malware Prevention:** Blocking malware before execution
- **Malware Detection:** Identifying active malware threats
- **Incident Response:** Responding to malware incidents

- **System Protection:** Maintaining system integrity

Implementation Checklist

Technical Prerequisites:

- Endpoint protection platform (EPP)
- Endpoint detection and response (EDR)
- Anti-malware solutions
- Application control system
- Network monitoring tools
- Sandboxing environment
- Threat intelligence platform
- Incident response system

Process Requirements:

- Deployment procedures
- Update management
- Quarantine protocols
- Response workflows
- Recovery procedures
- Exception handling
- Testing protocols
- Review schedules
- Documentation standards

Security Requirements:

- Real-time scanning
- Behavioral monitoring
- Signature updates
- Heuristic analysis
- Sandbox analysis
- Network isolation
- System restoration
- Incident reporting

Malware Defense Templates

Defense Configuration Template:
```
{
"defenseId": "unique_identifier",
"endpointProtection": {
"scanning": {
"realTime": "scan_settings",
"scheduled": "scan_frequency",
"onDemand": "trigger_conditions",
"exclusions": "exclusion_list"
},
"prevention": {
"heuristics": "detection_rules",
"behaviorMonitoring": "behavior_patterns",
"applicationControl": "control_rules",
"scriptBlocking": "script_policies"
```

},
"response": {
"quarantine": "quarantine_settings",
"remediation": "cleanup_procedures",
"isolation": "isolation_rules",
"recovery": "recovery_steps"
}
},
"networkDefense": {
"monitoring": {
"trafficAnalysis": "analysis_rules",
"protocolInspection": "inspection_config",
"threatDetection": "detection_settings",
"alerting": "alert_conditions"
},
"prevention": {
"filtering": "filter_rules",
"blocking": "block_criteria",
"sandboxing": "sandbox_config",
"networkIsolation": "isolation_policies"
}
},
"management": {
"updates": "update_schedule",
"reporting": "report_requirements",
"metrics": "measurement_criteria",
"review": "review_frequency"
},
"compliance": {
"requirements": ["PCI", "HIPAA", "SOX"],
"documentation": "required_docs",

"auditTrail": "audit_specs",
"exceptions": "exception_list"
}
}

CIS CONTROLS IN PRACTICE

Defense Configuration Form

Defense Information

Defense ID: _____

Endpoint Protection - Scanning

Real-Time Scanning: _____
Scheduled Scanning Frequency: _____
On-Demand Scanning: _____
Exclusions: _____

Endpoint Protection - Prevention

Heuristics: _____
Behavior Monitoring: _____
Application Control: _____
Script Blocking: _____

Endpoint Protection - Response

Quarantine Settings: _____
Remediation Procedures: _____
Isolation Rules: _____
Recovery Steps: _____

Network Defense - Monitoring

Traffic Analysis: _____
Protocol Inspection: _____
Threat Detection: _____
Alerting: _____

Network Defense - Prevention

Filtering Rules: _____
Blocking Criteria: _____
Sandboxing Configuration: _____
Network Isolation Policies: _____

Management

Updates: _____
Reporting: _____
Metrics: _____
Review Schedule: _____

Compliance

Requirements: [PCI | HIPAA | SOX]
Documentation: _____
Audit Trail: _____
Exceptions: _____

Implementation Steps

Phase 1: Foundation Setup (Weeks 1-6)

1. Infrastructure Preparation

- Deploy EPP solution
- Configure EDR
- Set up monitoring
- Implement sandboxing
- Configure reporting

2. Policy Development

- Define scanning policies
- Create response procedures
- Establish workflows
- Document standards
- Set up automation

Phase 2: Protection Implementation (Weeks 7-12)

1. Endpoint Protection

- Deploy agents
- Configure policies
- Implement controls
- Test effectiveness
- Document baseline

2. Network Defense

- Configure monitoring
- Implement filtering
- Set up isolation
- Test controls
- Validate protection

Phase 3: Operational Integration (Weeks 13-18)

1. Response Integration

- Connect systems
- Implement workflows
- Configure automation
- Set up reporting
- Test procedures

2. Program Optimization

- Fine-tune detection
- Enhance response
- Improve recovery
- Update documentation
- Validate effectiveness

Tools and Resources

Endpoint Protection Platforms:

- **CrowdStrike Falcon**
- **Features:** Next-gen antivirus, EDR
- **Use case:** Enterprise endpoint protection
- **Key capabilities:** AI-powered detection, response

- **Microsoft Defender for Endpoint**
- **Implementation scope:** Endpoint security
- **Key features:** Advanced threat protection
- **Integration capabilities:** Microsoft ecosystem

Network Defense Tools:

- **Palo Alto Networks Cortex XDR**
- **Features:** Extended detection and response
- **Use case:** Advanced threat detection
- **Key capabilities:** Behavioral analytics

- **FireEye Endpoint Security**
- **Implementation scope:** Malware protection
- **Key features:** Multi-engine detection
- **Integration points:** Security infrastructure

Management Platforms:

- **Tanium**
- **Features:** Endpoint management, security
- **Use case:** Enterprise endpoint control
- **Integration capabilities:** Security tools

- **VMware Carbon Black Cloud**
- **Key modules:** Prevention, detection, response
- **Integration points:** Security solutions
- **Automation features:** Response automation

Control 11: Data Recovery- Comprehensive Implementation Guide

Control Overview

Control 11 focuses on establishing and maintaining data recovery practices sufficient to restore in-scope enterprise assets to a pre-incident and trusted state. This control ensures organizations can recover from data loss or corruption events while maintaining business continuity. Primary goals include:

- **Backup Management:** Maintaining comprehensive data backups
- **Recovery Planning:** Establishing efficient recovery procedures

- **Data Validation:** Ensuring backup integrity and usability
- **Business Continuity:** Minimizing operational impact

Implementation Checklist

Technical Prerequisites:

- Backup infrastructure
- Storage solutions
- Recovery platforms
- Testing environment
- Monitoring tools
- Automation systems
- Validation tools
- Restoration infrastructure

Process Requirements:

- Backup policies
- Recovery procedures
- Testing schedules
- Validation protocols
- Documentation standards
- Review processes
- Incident procedures
- Training requirements
- Compliance validation

Security Requirements:

- Encryption standards
- Access controls
- Integrity checks
- Monitoring requirements
- Alert thresholds
- Security testing
- Incident response
- Compliance mapping

Data Recovery Templates

Recovery Plan Template:
```
{
"planId": "unique_identifier",
"backupStrategy": {
"configuration": {
"frequency": "backup_schedule",
"type": ["Full", "Differential", "Incremental"],
"retention": "retention_period",
"location": "storage_details"
},
"dataScope": {
"systems": "system_list",
"priorities": "priority_levels",
"dependencies": "dependency_map",
"exclusions": "exclusion_list"
```

```
},
"security": {
"encryption": "encryption_settings",
"access": "access_controls",
"monitoring": "monitoring_config",
"validation": "validation_rules"
}
},
"recoveryProcedures": {
"priorities": {
"critical": "recovery_time_objectives",
"important": "recovery_point_objectives",
"normal": "standard_recovery_times"
},
"steps": {
"preparation": "prep_procedures",
"execution": "recovery_steps",
"validation": "validation_process",
"documentation": "required_docs"
}
},
"testing": {
"schedule": "test_frequency",
"scenarios": "test_cases",
"validation": "success_criteria",
"reporting": "report_requirements"
},
"compliance": {
"requirements": ["SOX", "HIPAA", "PCI"],
"documentation": "required_records",
"auditTrail": "audit_requirements",
```

"verification": "verification_process"
}
}

CHAPTER 6: IMPLEMENTING CONTINUOUS MONITORING AND DEFENSE...

Recovery Plan Form

Plan Information

Plan ID: _____

Backup Strategy - Configuration

Frequency: _____
Type: [Full | Differential | Incremental]
Retention Period: _____
Location: _____

Backup Strategy - Data Scope

Systems: _____
Priorities: _____
Dependencies: _____
Exclusions: _____

Backup Strategy - Security

Encryption: _____
Access Controls: _____
Monitoring: _____
Validation: _____

Recovery Procedures - Priorities

Critical: _____
Important: _____
Normal: _____

Recovery Procedures - Steps

Preparation: _____
Execution: _____
Validation: _____
Documentation: _____

Testing

Schedule: _____
Scenarios: _____
Validation: _____
Reporting: _____

Compliance

Requirements: [SOX | HIPAA | PCI]
Documentation: _____
Audit Trail: _____
Verification: _____

Implementation Steps

Phase 1: Foundation Setup (Weeks 1-6)

1. Infrastructure Preparation

- Deploy backup systems
- Configure storage
- Set up monitoring
- Implement automation
- Configure validation

2. Policy Development

- Define backup policies
- Create recovery procedures
- Establish workflows
- Document standards
- Set up testing

Phase 2: Implementation (Weeks 7-12)

1. Backup Configuration

- Configure schedules
- Set up retention
- Implement security
- Test processes
- Validate backups

2. Recovery Setup

- Define procedures
- Configure automation
- Set up testing
- Implement validation
- Document processes

Phase 3: Operational Integration (Weeks 13-18)

1. Process Integration

- Connect systems
- Implement workflows
- Configure reporting
- Set up reviews
- Test procedures

2. Program Optimization

- Fine-tune backups
- Enhance recovery
- Improve validation
- Update documentation
- Validate effectiveness

Tools and Resources

Backup Solutions:

- **Veeam Backup & Replication**
- **Features:** Enterprise backup, replication
- **Use case:** Comprehensive data protection
- **Key capabilities:** Automated recovery testing

- **Commvault Complete Backup & Recovery**
- **Implementation scope:** Enterprise backup
- **Key features:** Unified data protection
- **Integration capabilities:** Cloud platforms

Storage Platforms:

- **Dell EMC Data Domain**
- **Features:** Deduplication storage
- **Use case:** Backup target storage
- **Key capabilities:** Data reduction, replication

- **NetApp ONTAP**
- **Implementation scope:** Enterprise storage
- **Key features:** Snapshot, replication
- **Integration points:** Backup solutions

Recovery Management:

- **Rubrik**
- **Features:** Cloud data management
- **Use case:** Enterprise recovery
- **Integration capabilities:** Multiple platforms

- **Cohesity DataProtect**
- **Key modules:** Backup, recovery, automation
- **Integration points:** Enterprise systems
- **Automation features:** Recovery orchestration

Control 12: Network Infrastructure Management- Comprehensive Implementation Guide

Control Overview

Control 12 focuses on establishing and maintaining a secure network infrastructure through proper configuration, monitoring, and lifecycle management. This control ensures organizations maintain the security and reliability of their network infrastructure components. Primary goals include:

- **Network Security:** Maintaining secure network configurations
- **Infrastructure Management:** Managing network device lifecycle

- **Configuration Control:** Ensuring proper device configurations
- **Performance Monitoring:** Maintaining network reliability

Implementation Checklist

Technical Prerequisites:

- Network management system
- Configuration management database
- Monitoring platform
- Automation tools
- Change management system
- Backup solutions
- Documentation platform
- Testing environment

Process Requirements:

- Configuration standards
- Change procedures
- Monitoring protocols
- Review schedules
- Backup procedures
- Update policies
- Testing requirements
- Documentation standards
- Compliance validation

Security Requirements:

- Access control policies
- Authentication standards
- Encryption requirements
- Monitoring rules
- Alert thresholds
- Incident procedures
- Compliance mapping
- Security testing

Network Management Templates

Infrastructure Configuration Template:
```
{
"deviceId": "unique_identifier",
"networkDevice": {
"configuration": {
"type": ["Router", "Switch", "Firewall"],
"model": "device_model",
"location": "device_location",
"role": "device_function"
},
"security": {
"authentication": "auth_methods",
"access": "access_controls",
"encryption": "crypto_settings",
"hardening": "security_configs"
```

},
"monitoring": {
"performance": "metrics_config",
"availability": "uptime_requirements",
"alerts": "alert_thresholds",
"logging": "log_settings"
}
},
"maintenance": {
"updates": {
"schedule": "update_frequency",
"process": "update_procedures",
"testing": "test_requirements",
"rollback": "rollback_plan"
},
"backup": {
"frequency": "backup_schedule",
"retention": "retention_period",
"verification": "verify_process",
"restoration": "restore_steps"
}
},
"compliance": {
"standards": ["PCI", "NIST", "ISO"],
"requirements": "compliance_specs",
"validation": "audit_process",
"documentation": "required_docs"
}
}

CHAPTER 6: IMPLEMENTING CONTINUOUS MONITORING AND DEFENSE...

Infrastructure Configuration Form

Device Information

Device ID: _____

Network Device - Configuration

Type: [Router | Switch | Firewall]
Model: _____
Location: _____
Role: _____

Network Device - Security

Authentication: _____
Access Controls: _____
Encryption: _____
Hardening: _____

Network Device - Monitoring

Performance Metrics: _____
Availability Requirements: _____
Alerts: _____
Logging: _____

Maintenance - Updates

Schedule: _____
Process: _____
Testing Requirements: _____
Rollback Plan: _____

Maintenance - Backup

Frequency: _____
Retention Period: _____
Verification Process: _____
Restoration Steps: _____

Compliance

Standards: [PCI | NIST | ISO]
Requirements: _____
Validation Process: _____
Documentation: _____

Implementation Steps

Phase 1: Foundation Setup (Weeks 1-6)

1. Infrastructure Assessment

- Document current state
- Identify gaps
- Define requirements
- Plan improvements
- Set priorities

2. Standards Development

- Create configuration standards
- Define security policies
- Establish procedures
- Document requirements
- Set baselines

Phase 2: Implementation (Weeks 7-12)

1. Security Implementation

- Configure access controls
- Implement authentication
- Set up encryption
- Deploy monitoring
- Test controls

2. Management Setup

- Deploy management tools
- Configure automation
- Set up backups
- Implement changes
- Test procedures

Phase 3: Operational Integration (Weeks 13-18)

1. Process Integration

- Connect systems
- Implement workflows
- Configure reporting
- Set up reviews
- Test integration

2. Program Optimization

- Fine-tune configurations
- Enhance monitoring
- Improve automation
- Update documentation
- Validate effectiveness

Tools and Resources

Network Management Platforms:

- **Cisco DNA Center**
- **Features:** Network automation, assurance
- **Use case:** Enterprise network management
- **Key capabilities:** Intent-based networking

- **SolarWinds Network Configuration Manager**
- **Implementation scope:** Configuration management
- **Key features:** Automation, compliance
- **Integration capabilities:** Network monitoring

Monitoring Solutions:

- **PRTG Network Monitor**
- **Features:** Comprehensive monitoring
- **Use case:** Infrastructure monitoring
- **Key capabilities:** Performance tracking

- **Nagios XI**
- **Implementation scope:** Network monitoring
- **Key features:** Alert management
- **Integration points:** Management systems

Security Tools:

- **Cisco ISE**
- **Features:** Network access control
- **Use case:** Security enforcement
- **Integration capabilities:** Network infrastructure

- **Fortinet FortiManager**
- **Key modules:** Security management
- **Integration points:** Security devices
- **Automation features:** Policy deployment

Control 13: Network Monitoring and Defense- Comprehensive Implementation Guide

Control Overview

Control 13 focuses on operating and maintaining processes and tools to establish and maintain comprehensive network monitoring and defense against security threats. This control ensures organizations can detect, prevent, and respond to network-based attacks. Primary goals include:

- **Network Visibility:** Maintaining comprehensive network awareness

- **Threat Detection:** Identifying security threats in real-time
- **Incident Response:** Responding to network-based attacks
- **Defense Implementation:** Deploying effective security controls

Implementation Checklist

Technical Prerequisites:

- Network Detection and Response (NDR)
- Security Information and Event Management (SIEM)
- Intrusion Detection/Prevention Systems
- Network Traffic Analysis tools
- Threat Intelligence platform
- Packet capture capability
- Flow monitoring tools
- Incident response platform

Process Requirements:

- Monitoring procedures
- Alert workflows
- Response protocols
- Review schedules
- Investigation procedures
- Tuning processes
- Documentation standards
- Training requirements

- Incident playbooks

Security Requirements:

- Detection rules
- Alert thresholds
- Response procedures
- Investigation standards
- Containment protocols
- Evidence collection
- Threat hunting
- Compliance validation

Network Monitoring Templates

Defense Configuration Template:
{
"monitoringId": "unique_identifier",
"networkDefense": {
"detection": {
"sensors": "sensor_placement",
"coverage": "monitoring_scope",
"methods": "detection_techniques",
"baselines": "normal_behavior"
},
"analysis": {
"trafficAnalysis": "analysis_rules",

```
"behaviorModeling": "behavior_patterns",
"threatHunting": "hunting_procedures",
"forensics": "investigation_methods"
},
"response": {
"alerting": "alert_conditions",
"containment": "containment_procedures",
"remediation": "cleanup_steps",
"recovery": "recovery_processes"
}
},
"integrations": {
"tools": {
"siem": "integration_config",
"soar": "automation_rules",
"ticketing": "ticket_workflow",
"reporting": "report_config"
},
"intelligence": {
"sources": "intel_feeds",
"correlation": "correlation_rules",
"enrichment": "enrichment_process",
"sharing": "sharing_protocols"
}
},
"compliance": {
"requirements": ["PCI", "HIPAA", "SOX"],
"monitoring": "compliance_checks",
"reporting": "report_requirements",
"validation": "audit_procedures"
}
```

CHAPTER 6: IMPLEMENTING CONTINUOUS MONITORING AND DEFENSE...

}

CIS CONTROLS IN PRACTICE

Defense Configuration Form

Monitoring Information

Monitoring ID: _____

Network Defense - Detection

Sensors Placement: _____
Coverage Scope: _____
Detection Methods: _____
Baselines (Normal Behavior): _____

Network Defense - Analysis

Traffic Analysis Rules: _____
Behavior Modeling Patterns: _____
Threat Hunting Procedures: _____
Forensics Investigation Methods: _____

Network Defense - Response

Alerting Conditions: _____
Containment Procedures: _____
Remediation Steps: _____
Recovery Processes: _____

Integrations - Tools

SIEM Integration Config: _____
SOAR Automation Rules: _____
Ticketing Workflow: _____
Reporting Configuration: _____

Integrations - Intelligence

Intel Sources: _____
Correlation Rules: _____
Enrichment Process: _____
Sharing Protocols: _____

Compliance

Requirements: [PCI | HIPAA | SOX]
Monitoring Checks: _____
Reporting Requirements: _____
Validation (Audit Procedures): _____

Implementation Steps

Phase 1: Foundation Setup (Weeks 1-6)

1. Infrastructure Preparation

- Deploy monitoring tools
- Configure sensors
- Set up analysis
- Implement storage
- Configure reporting

2. Policy Development

- Define monitoring policies
- Create response procedures
- Establish workflows
- Document standards
- Set up automation

Phase 2: Detection Implementation (Weeks 7-12)

1. Monitoring Setup

- Configure detection
- Implement analysis
- Set up alerting
- Test effectiveness
- Validate coverage

2. Response Integration

- Configure workflows
- Implement playbooks
- Set up automation
- Test procedures
- Validate response

Phase 3: Operational Integration (Weeks 13-18)

1. Process Integration

- Connect systems
- Implement correlation
- Configure reporting
- Set up reviews
- Test procedures

2. Program Optimization

- Fine-tune detection
- Enhance response
- Improve analysis
- Update documentation
- Validate effectiveness

Tools and Resources

Network Monitoring Platforms:

- **Cisco Stealthwatch**
- **Features:** Network visibility, threat detection
- **Use case:** Enterprise network monitoring
- **Key capabilities:** Behavioral analytics

- **Darktrace Enterprise Immune System**
- **Implementation scope:** Network detection
- **Key features:** AI-powered analysis
- **Integration capabilities:** Security tools

Analysis Tools:

- **ExtraHop Reveal(x)**
- **Features:** NDR capabilities
- **Use case:** Advanced threat detection
- **Key capabilities:** Real-time analysis

- **Vectra Cognito Platform**
- **Implementation scope:** AI-driven detection
- **Key features:** Automated threat detection
- **Integration points:** Security infrastructure

Defense Solutions:

- **Palo Alto Networks**
- **Features:** Next-gen firewall, threat prevention
- **Use case:** Network defense
- **Integration capabilities:** Security ecosystem

- **Fortinet FortiGate**
- **Key modules:** UTM, threat protection
- **Integration points:** Security infrastructure
- **Automation features:** Response automation

Control 14: Security Awareness and Skills Training- Comprehensive Implementation Guide

Control Overview

Control 14 focuses on establishing and maintaining a comprehensive security awareness and training program for all enterprise personnel. This control ensures organizations develop and maintain a security-conscious workforce. Primary goals include:

- **Awareness Development:** Building security consciousness
- **Skills Enhancement:** Developing technical security skills
- **Behavior Change:** Promoting secure practices

- **Compliance Training:** Meeting regulatory requirements

Implementation Checklist

Technical Prerequisites:

- Learning Management System (LMS)
- Training content platform
- Assessment tools
- Phishing simulation platform
- Progress tracking system
- Reporting tools
- Content management system
- Automation platform

Process Requirements:

- Training curriculum
- Assessment procedures
- Tracking methods
- Review schedules
- Documentation standards
- Feedback processes
- Compliance validation
- Update procedures
- Effectiveness metrics

Program Requirements:

- Role-based training
- Baseline awareness
- Technical skills development
- Compliance training
- Incident response training
- Social engineering awareness
- Security best practices
- Performance measurement

Training Program Templates

Training Plan Template:
```
{
"programId": "unique_identifier",
"trainingStructure": {
"baseline": {
"content": "awareness_topics",
"frequency": "delivery_schedule",
"duration": "time_requirements",
"assessment": "evaluation_methods"
},
"roleBased": {
"technicalStaff": "technical_curriculum",
"management": "leadership_topics",
"general": "user_awareness",
"specialized": "role_specific"
```

CHAPTER 6: IMPLEMENTING CONTINUOUS MONITORING AND DEFENSE...

```
},
"delivery": {
"methods": ["Online", "Classroom", "Simulation"],
"materials": "content_types",
"scheduling": "delivery_timeline",
"tracking": "completion_monitoring"
}
},
"assessment": {
"methods": {
"testing": "test_formats",
"simulation": "practical_exercises",
"evaluation": "performance_metrics",
"feedback": "collection_methods"
},
"compliance": {
"requirements": "compliance_standards",
"documentation": "required_records",
"reporting": "report_formats",
"validation": "audit_procedures"
}
},
"measurement": {
"metrics": {
"completion": "tracking_methods",
"effectiveness": "success_measures",
"behavior": "change_indicators",
"impact": "business_outcomes"
},
"reporting": {
"frequency": "report_schedule",
```

"audience": "stakeholders",
"format": "report_types",
"distribution": "delivery_methods"
}
}
}

CHAPTER 6: IMPLEMENTING CONTINUOUS MONITORING AND DEFENSE...

Training Plan Form

Program Information

Program ID: _____

Training Structure - Baseline

Content (Awareness Topics): _____
Frequency (Delivery Schedule): _____
Duration: _____
Assessment Methods: _____

Training Structure - Role-Based

Technical Staff Curriculum: _____
Management Topics: _____
General User Awareness: _____
Specialized Role-Specific Training: _____

Training Structure - Delivery

Methods: [Online | Classroom | Simulation]
Materials: _____
Scheduling Timeline: _____
Tracking (Completion Monitoring): _____

Assessment Methods

Testing Formats: _____
Simulation Exercises: _____
Evaluation Metrics: _____
Feedback Collection Methods: _____

Compliance

Requirements: _____
Documentation: _____
Reporting Formats: _____
Validation (Audit Procedures): _____

Measurement - Metrics

Completion Tracking Methods: _____
Effectiveness Success Measures: _____
Behavior Change Indicators: _____
Impact on Business Outcomes: _____

Measurement - Reporting

Frequency: _____
Audience (Stakeholders): _____
Format (Report Types): _____
Distribution Methods: _____

Implementation Steps

Phase 1: Program Development (Weeks 1-6)

1. Content Development

- Create training materials
- Develop assessments
- Build simulations
- Establish baseline
- Design curriculum

2. Platform Setup

- Deploy LMS
- Configure tracking
- Set up reporting
- Implement automation
- Test delivery

Phase 2: Implementation (Weeks 7-12)

1. Training Rollout

- Launch awareness program
- Conduct assessments
- Track completion
- Monitor effectiveness
- Gather feedback

2. Skills Development

- Deliver technical training
- Conduct simulations
- Implement exercises
- Test knowledge
- Document progress

Phase 3: Program Management (Weeks 13-18)

1. Effectiveness Monitoring

- Track metrics
- Analyze results
- Adjust content
- Update materials
- Validate impact

2. Continuous Improvement

- Gather feedback
- Update content
- Enhance delivery
- Improve assessment
- Optimize program

Tools and Resources

Learning Management Systems:

- **KnowBe4**
- **Features:** Security awareness training, phishing simulation
- **Use case:** Enterprise security training
- **Key capabilities:** Content management, automation

- **SAP Litmos**
- **Implementation scope:** Corporate training
- **Key features:** Content delivery, tracking
- **Integration capabilities:** HR systems

Simulation Platforms:

- **Cofense PhishMe**
- **Features:** Phishing simulation, reporting
- **Use case:** Social engineering awareness
- **Key capabilities:** Behavior tracking

- **Proofpoint Security Awareness Training**
- **Implementation scope:** Security awareness
- **Key features:** Customized training
- **Integration points:** Email security

Assessment Tools:

- **Questionmark**
- **Features:** Assessment management
- **Use case:** Knowledge testing
- **Integration capabilities:** LMS platforms

- **Canvas LMS**
- **Key modules:** Course management
- **Integration points:** Training systems
- **Automation features:** Progress tracking

Chapter 7: Implementing Governance and Organizational Controls (Controls 15-18)

Control 15: Service Provider Management- Comprehensive Implementation Guide

Control Overview

Control 15 focuses on developing and maintaining an enterprise process to evaluate and manage risks associated with service providers. This control ensures organizations effectively manage third-party relationships and associated security risks. Primary goals include:

- **Provider Assessment:** Evaluating service provider security
- **Risk Management:** Managing third-party security risks
- **Compliance Validation:** Ensuring provider compliance
- **Contract Management:** Maintaining security requirements

Implementation Checklist

Technical Prerequisites:

- Vendor management platform
- Risk assessment tools
- Contract management system
- Monitoring solutions
- Assessment framework
- Documentation system
- Compliance tracking
- Reporting platform

Process Requirements:

- Assessment procedures
- Evaluation criteria
- Review schedules
- Monitoring protocols
- Documentation standards
- Reporting requirements
- Incident procedures
- Compliance validation
- Contract templates

Governance Requirements:

- Risk thresholds

- Security standards
- Compliance requirements
- Performance metrics
- Review criteria
- Escalation procedures
- Exit strategies
- Oversight mechanisms

Service Provider Management Templates

Provider Assessment Template:
```
{
"providerId": "unique_identifier",
"assessmentFramework": {
"initialAssessment": {
"security": "security_requirements",
"compliance": "compliance_standards",
"capabilities": "service_capabilities",
"risks": "risk_factors"
},
"ongoingMonitoring": {
"performance": "metrics_tracking",
"compliance": "compliance_monitoring",
"incidents": "incident_tracking",
"changes": "change_management"
},
"riskManagement": {
"classification": "risk_levels",
```

```
"mitigation": "control_requirements",
"monitoring": "risk_tracking",
"reporting": "risk_reporting"
}
},
"contractManagement": {
"requirements": {
"security": "security_controls",
"service": "service_levels",
"compliance": "compliance_requirements",
"reporting": "report_specifications"
},
"oversight": {
"governance": "oversight_structure",
"reviews": "review_schedule",
"audits": "audit_requirements",
"escalation": "escalation_process"
}
},
"compliance": {
"standards": ["SOC2", "ISO27001", "PCI"],
"validation": "validation_process",
"documentation": "required_evidence",
"reporting": "compliance_reporting"
}
}
```

CIS CONTROLS IN PRACTICE

Provider Assessment Form

Provider Information

Provider ID: _____

Assessment Framework - Initial Assessment

Security Requirements: _____
Compliance Standards: _____
Service Capabilities: _____
Risk Factors: _____

Assessment Framework - Ongoing Monitoring

Performance Metrics Tracking: _____
Compliance Monitoring: _____
Incident Tracking: _____
Change Management: _____

Assessment Framework - Risk Management

Risk Classification Levels: _____
Mitigation Controls: _____
Risk Monitoring: _____
Risk Reporting: _____

Contract Management - Requirements

Security Controls: _____
Service Levels: _____
Compliance Requirements: _____
Reporting Specifications: _____

Contract Management - Oversight

Governance Structure: _____
Review Schedule: _____
Audit Requirements: _____
Escalation Process: _____

Compliance

Standards: [SOC2 | ISO27001 | PCI]
Validation Process: _____
Documentation: _____
Compliance Reporting: _____

Implementation Steps

Phase 1: Program Development (Weeks 1-6)

1. Framework Development

- Create assessment criteria
- Define risk thresholds
- Establish procedures
- Document standards
- Design workflows

2. Tool Implementation

- Deploy management platform
- Configure assessment tools
- Set up monitoring
- Implement reporting
- Test processes

Phase 2: Provider Assessment (Weeks 7-12)

1. Initial Assessment

- Conduct evaluations
- Perform risk analysis
- Document findings
- Establish baselines
- Create reports

2. Control Implementation

- Define requirements
- Implement monitoring
- Set up reporting
- Establish reviews
- Test effectiveness

Phase 3: Ongoing Management (Weeks 13-18)

1. Monitoring Integration

- Configure continuous monitoring
- Implement alerts
- Set up reviews
- Establish reporting
- Test procedures

2. Program Optimization

- Fine-tune assessments
- Enhance monitoring
- Improve reporting
- Update documentation
- Validate effectiveness

Tools and Resources

Vendor Management Platforms:

- **OneTrust Vendorpedia**
- **Features:** Third-party risk management
- **Use case:** Vendor security assessment
- **Key capabilities:** Risk monitoring, automation

- **ProcessUnity VRM**
- **Implementation scope:** Vendor risk management
- **Key features:** Assessment automation
- **Integration capabilities:** GRC platforms

Risk Assessment Tools:

- **BitSight Security Ratings**
- **Features:** Security rating platform
- **Use case:** Continuous monitoring
- **Key capabilities:** Real-time assessment

- **SecurityScorecard**
- **Implementation scope:** Security ratings
- **Key features:** Continuous monitoring
- **Integration points:** Risk management

Management Platforms:

- **ServiceNow Vendor Risk Management**
- **Features:** Integrated risk management
- **Use case:** Enterprise vendor management
- **Integration capabilities:** ITSM platforms

- **Aravo Enterprise**
- **Key modules:** Third-party management
- **Integration points:** Enterprise systems
- **Automation features:** Workflow automation

Control 16: Application Software Security- Comprehensive Implementation Guide

Control Overview

Control 16 focuses on managing the security lifecycle of all in-house developed and acquired software to prevent, detect, and remediate security vulnerabilities. This control ensures organizations maintain robust application security throughout the software development lifecycle. Primary goals include:

- **Secure Development:** Implementing secure coding practices
- **Security Testing:** Validating application security

- **Vulnerability Management:** Identifying and fixing vulnerabilities
- **Continuous Monitoring:** Maintaining application security posture

Implementation Checklist

Technical Prerequisites:

- Static Application Security Testing (SAST)
- Dynamic Application Security Testing (DAST)
- Software Composition Analysis (SCA)
- Security testing framework
- Code review platform
- Vulnerability scanners
- CI/CD security tools
- Monitoring solutions

Process Requirements:

- Secure SDLC procedures
- Testing protocols
- Review schedules
- Release criteria
- Documentation standards
- Incident procedures
- Change management
- Training requirements
- Compliance validation

Security Requirements:

- Security standards
- Testing requirements
- Code review criteria
- Release gates
- Monitoring rules
- Response procedures
- Compliance mapping
- Risk thresholds

Application Security Templates

Security Framework Template:
```
{
"applicationId": "unique_identifier",
"securityControls": {
"development": {
"coding": "secure_coding_standards",
"reviews": "review_requirements",
"testing": "test_specifications",
"validation": "validation_criteria"
},
"testing": {
"static": "sast_configuration",
"dynamic": "dast_configuration",
"composition": "sca_requirements",
"penetration": "pentest_scope"
```

},
"deployment": {
"gates": "security_gates",
"monitoring": "monitoring_config",
"scanning": "scan_schedule",
"response": "incident_procedures"
}
},
"lifecycle": {
"phases": {
"planning": "security_requirements",
"development": "control_implementation",
"testing": "security_validation",
"deployment": "security_monitoring"
},
"maintenance": {
"updates": "patch_management",
"monitoring": "continuous_assessment",
"response": "incident_handling",
"review": "security_reviews"
}
},
"compliance": {
"standards": ["PCI-DSS", "OWASP", "NIST"],
"validation": "compliance_checks",
"documentation": "required_records",
"reporting": "compliance_reports"
}
}

CIS CONTROLS IN PRACTICE

Security Framework Form

Application Information

Application ID: _____

Security Controls - Development

Secure Coding Standards: _____
Review Requirements: _____
Testing Specifications: _____
Validation Criteria: _____

Security Controls - Testing

Static Analysis (SAST): _____
Dynamic Analysis (DAST): _____
Composition Analysis (SCA): _____
Penetration Test Scope: _____

Security Controls - Deployment

Security Gates: _____
Monitoring Configuration: _____
Scanning Schedule: _____
Incident Response Procedures: _____

Lifecycle - Phases

Planning (Security Requirements): _____
Development (Control Implementation): _____
Testing (Security Validation): _____
Deployment (Security Monitoring): _____

Lifecycle - Maintenance

Patch Management Updates: _____
Continuous Assessment Monitoring: _____
Incident Handling Response: _____
Security Reviews: _____

Compliance

Standards: [PCI-DSS | OWASP | NIST]
Validation Checks: _____
Documentation: _____
Compliance Reporting: _____

Implementation Steps

Phase 1: Foundation Setup (Weeks 1-6)

1. Infrastructure Preparation

- Deploy security tools
- Configure testing
- Set up monitoring
- Implement automation
- Configure reporting

2. Process Development

- Define security standards
- Create testing procedures
- Establish workflows
- Document requirements
- Set up training

Phase 2: Security Implementation (Weeks 7-12)

1. Development Integration

- Implement SAST
- Configure DAST
- Set up SCA
- Test integration
- Validate effectiveness

2. Process Integration

- Configure workflows
- Implement gates
- Set up monitoring
- Establish reviews
- Test procedures

Phase 3: Operational Integration (Weeks 13-18)

1. Continuous Monitoring

- Configure scanning
- Implement alerts
- Set up reporting
- Establish reviews
- Test effectiveness

2. Program Optimization

- Fine-tune testing
- Enhance detection
- Improve response
- Update documentation
- Validate controls

Tools and Resources

Application Security Testing:

- **Checkmarx CxSAST**
- **Features:** Static code analysis
- **Use case:** Secure development
- **Key capabilities:** Automated testing

- **Fortify WebInspect**
- **Implementation scope:** Dynamic testing
- **Key features:** Automated scanning
- **Integration capabilities:** CI/CD pipeline

Vulnerability Management:

- **Snyk**
- **Features:** SCA, vulnerability detection
- **Use case:** Dependency scanning
- **Key capabilities:** Automated remediation

- **Veracode**
- **Implementation scope:** Application security
- **Key features:** Complete testing suite
- **Integration points:** Development tools

Security Platforms:

- **SonarQube**
- **Features:** Code quality, security
- **Use case:** Continuous inspection
- **Integration capabilities:** DevOps tools

- **GitLab Security**
- **Key modules:** Security testing
- **Integration points:** Development pipeline
- **Automation features:** Security scanning

Control 17: Incident Response Management- Comprehensive Implementation Guide

Control Overview

Control 17 focuses on establishing and maintaining an incident response infrastructure and processes to detect, analyze, contain, and recover from security incidents. This control ensures organizations can effectively respond to and manage security incidents. Primary goals include:

- **Incident Detection:** Identifying security incidents quickly
- **Response Management:** Coordinating effective incident response

CHAPTER 7: IMPLEMENTING GOVERNANCE AND ORGANIZATIONAL...

- **Impact Mitigation:** Minimizing incident impact
- **Recovery Planning:** Ensuring business continuity

Implementation Checklist

Technical Prerequisites:

- Security Information and Event Management (SIEM)
- Incident Response Platform
- Forensics tools
- Case management system
- Communications platform
- Evidence collection tools
- Automation platform
- Documentation system

Process Requirements:

- Response procedures
- Escalation protocols
- Communication plans
- Recovery procedures
- Documentation standards
- Training requirements
- Review schedules
- Testing protocols
- Compliance validation

Incident Management Requirements:

- Detection criteria
- Classification standards
- Response playbooks
- Investigation procedures
- Containment strategies
- Recovery plans
- Reporting requirements
- Lessons learned process

Incident Response Templates

Response Plan Template:
```
{
"incidentId": "unique_identifier",
"responseFramework": {
"preparation": {
"resources": "required_resources",
"roles": "team_responsibilities",
"tools": "technical_requirements",
"training": "training_needs"
},
"detection": {
"sources": "detection_methods",
"criteria": "incident_criteria",
"triage": "initial_assessment",
"notification": "alert_procedures"
```

},
"response": {
"investigation": "investigation_steps",
"containment": "containment_strategies",
"eradication": "removal_procedures",
"recovery": "restoration_steps"
}
},
"management": {
"communication": {
"internal": "internal_procedures",
"external": "external_procedures",
"stakeholders": "communication_plan",
"escalation": "escalation_matrix"
},
"documentation": {
"evidence": "collection_procedures",
"timeline": "incident_tracking",
"actions": "response_documentation",
"decisions": "decision_tracking"
}
},
"compliance": {
"requirements": ["SOX", "HIPAA", "PCI"],
"reporting": "reporting_requirements",
"notification": "disclosure_requirements",
"retention": "retention_policies"
}
}

CIS CONTROLS IN PRACTICE

Response Plan Form

Incident Information

Incident ID: _____

Response Framework - Preparation

Required Resources: _____
Team Responsibilities: _____
Technical Requirements (Tools): _____
Training Needs: _____

Response Framework - Detection

Detection Sources: _____
Incident Criteria: _____
Initial Assessment (Triage): _____
Notification Procedures: _____

Response Framework - Response

Investigation Steps: _____
Containment Strategies: _____
Removal Procedures (Eradication): _____
Restoration Steps (Recovery): _____

Management - Communication

Internal Procedures: _____
External Procedures: _____
Stakeholder Communication Plan: _____
Escalation Matrix: _____

Management - Documentation

Evidence Collection Procedures: _____
Incident Tracking Timeline: _____
Response Actions Documentation: _____
Decision Tracking: _____

Compliance

Requirements: [SOX | HIPAA | PCI]
Reporting Requirements: _____
Disclosure Requirements (Notification): _____
Retention Policies: _____

Implementation Steps

Phase 1: Foundation Setup (Weeks 1-6)

1. Infrastructure Preparation

- Deploy response platform
- Configure tools
- Set up communication
- Implement automation
- Configure reporting

2. Process Development

- Create response procedures
- Define playbooks
- Establish workflows
- Document requirements
- Set up training

Phase 2: Response Implementation (Weeks 7-12)

1. Team Development

- Assign roles
- Conduct training
- Test procedures
- Validate capabilities
- Document processes

2. Process Integration

- Configure workflows
- Implement automation
- Set up reporting
- Establish reviews
- Test effectiveness

Phase 3: Program Optimization (Weeks 13-18)

1. Exercise Program

- Conduct simulations
- Test procedures
- Validate response
- Document lessons
- Improve processes

2. Continuous Improvement

- Review incidents
- Update procedures
- Enhance capabilities
- Improve documentation
- Validate effectiveness

Tools and Resources

Incident Response Platforms:

- **IBM Resilient**
- **Features:** Incident coordination
- **Use case:** Enterprise incident response
- **Key capabilities:** Automation, orchestration

- **ServiceNow Security Operations**
- **Implementation scope:** Security operations
- **Key features:** Incident management
- **Integration capabilities:** ITSM integration

Forensics Tools:

- **EnCase Forensic**
- **Features:** Digital forensics
- **Use case:** Incident investigation
- **Key capabilities:** Evidence collection

- **Magnet AXIOM**
- **Implementation scope:** Digital investigation
- **Key features:** Advanced analysis
- **Integration points:** Evidence management

Communication Platforms:

- **PagerDuty**
- **Features:** Incident alerting
- **Use case:** Response coordination
- **Integration capabilities:** Multiple platforms

- **Slack for Incident Response**
- **Key modules:** Communication
- **Integration points:** Response tools
- **Automation features:** Workflow automation

Control 18: Penetration Testing- Comprehensive Implementation Guide

Control Overview

Control 18 tests the overall strength of an organization's security posture through penetration testing and red team exercises. This control ensures organizations regularly validate their security effectiveness through simulated attacks. Primary goals include:

- **Security Validation:** Testing security control effectiveness
- **Vulnerability Discovery:** Identifying security weaknesses
- **Risk Assessment:** Evaluating security posture

CHAPTER 7: IMPLEMENTING GOVERNANCE AND ORGANIZATIONAL...

- **Improvement Planning:** Enhancing security controls

Implementation Checklist

Technical Prerequisites:

- Penetration testing tools
- Vulnerability scanners
- Network mapping tools
- Exploitation frameworks
- Testing environment
- Documentation platform
- Reporting system
- Tracking solution

Process Requirements:

- Testing methodology
- Scope definition
- Authorization procedures
- Communication plans
- Documentation standards
- Review processes
- Reporting requirements
- Remediation tracking
- Compliance validation

Testing Requirements:

- Rules of engagement
- Target identification
- Testing boundaries
- Success criteria
- Safety measures
- Evidence collection
- Reporting standards
- Follow-up procedures

Penetration Testing Templates

Testing Framework Template:
```
{
"testingId": "unique_identifier",
"planningPhase": {
"scope": {
"targets": "target_systems",
"boundaries": "test_limitations",
"objectives": "test_goals",
"timeline": "schedule_details"
},
"authorization": {
"approvals": "required_authorizations",
"documentation": "legal_requirements",
"communication": "notification_plan",
"emergency": "emergency_procedures"
```

CHAPTER 7: IMPLEMENTING GOVERNANCE AND ORGANIZATIONAL...

},
"methodology": {
"approach": "testing_methods",
"tools": "approved_tools",
"techniques": "allowed_techniques",
"safeguards": "safety_measures"
}
},
"executionPhase": {
"reconnaissance": {
"passive": "passive_methods",
"active": "active_methods",
"documentation": "findings_recording",
"analysis": "initial_assessment"
},
"testing": {
"vulnerability": "vulnerability_assessment",
"exploitation": "exploitation_attempts",
"postExploitation": "post_exploit_actions",
"documentation": "evidence_collection"
}
},
"reporting": {
"findings": {
"vulnerabilities": "identified_issues",
"risks": "risk_assessment",
"recommendations": "improvement_suggestions",
"priorities": "remediation_priorities"
},
"documentation": {
"technical": "technical_details",

"executive": "executive_summary",
"evidence": "supporting_evidence",
"metrics": "test_metrics"
}
}
}

CHAPTER 7: IMPLEMENTING GOVERNANCE AND ORGANIZATIONAL...

Testing Framework Form

Testing Information

Testing ID: _____

Planning Phase - Scope

Target Systems: _____
Test Limitations: _____
Test Goals: _____
Schedule Details: _____

Planning Phase - Authorization

Required Authorizations: _____
Legal Requirements Documentation: _____
Notification Plan: _____
Emergency Procedures: _____

Planning Phase - Methodology

Testing Methods (Approach): _____
Approved Tools: _____
Allowed Techniques: _____
Safety Measures (Safeguards): _____

Execution Phase - Reconnaissance

Passive Methods: _____
Active Methods: _____
Findings Documentation: _____
Initial Assessment (Analysis): _____

Execution Phase - Testing

Vulnerability Assessment: _____
Exploitation Attempts: _____
Post-Exploitation Actions: _____
Evidence Collection Documentation: _____

Reporting - Findings

Identified Vulnerabilities: _____
Risk Assessment: _____
Improvement Recommendations: _____
Remediation Priorities: _____

Reporting - Documentation

Technical Details: _____
Executive Summary: _____
Supporting Evidence: _____
Test Metrics: _____

Implementation Steps

Phase 1: Program Development (Weeks 1-6)

1. Framework Development

- Define methodology
- Create procedures
- Establish scope
- Document requirements
- Set up processes

2. Infrastructure Preparation

- Configure testing environment
- Set up tools
- Implement safeguards
- Configure monitoring
- Test procedures

Phase 2: Testing Implementation (Weeks 7-12)

1. Initial Assessment

- Conduct reconnaissance
- Map infrastructure
- Identify targets
- Document findings
- Plan approach

2. Testing Execution

- Perform testing
- Document findings
- Track progress
- Maintain communication
- Ensure safety

Phase 3: Program Management (Weeks 13-18)

1. Reporting Integration

- Generate reports
- Present findings
- Track remediation
- Monitor progress
- Validate fixes

2. Program Optimization

- Review effectiveness
- Update methodology
- Enhance processes
- Improve documentation
- Validate approach

Tools and Resources

Penetration Testing Platforms:

- **Metasploit Framework**
- **Features:** Exploitation framework
- **Use case:** Security testing
- **Key capabilities:** Vulnerability testing

- **Burp Suite Professional**
- **Implementation scope:** Web application testing
- **Key features:** Security assessment
- **Integration capabilities:** Testing workflow

Reconnaissance Tools:

- **Nmap**
- **Features:** Network discovery
- **Use case:** Infrastructure mapping
- **Key capabilities:** Port scanning

- **Maltego**
- **Implementation scope:** Information gathering
- **Key features:** Data correlation
- **Integration points:** OSINT sources

Testing Management:

- **PlexTrac**
- **Features:** Pentest management
- **Use case:** Testing coordination
- **Integration capabilities:** Reporting tools

- **Cobalt Platform**
- **Key modules:** Pentest management
- **Integration points:** Development tools
- **Automation features:** Workflow management

Chapter 8: Understanding and Applying Implementation Groups (IGs)

Introduction to Implementation Groups

Implementation Groups represent one of the most significant advancements in the CIS Controls framework. They provide organizations with a practical approach to security implementation based on their resources, capabilities, and risk profile. This concept fundamentally changes how organizations implement security control by offering a structured, progressive pathway to enhanced security posture.

The purpose of Implementation Groups extends beyond simple categorization. **These groups provide organizations with realistic, achievable security objectives while acknowledging varying levels of resources and capabilities.** By categorizing controls into three distinct implementation groups, the framework helps organizations focus on the most critical security measures appropriate for their situation rather than attempting to implement all controls simultaneously without adequate preparation or resources.

Implementation Groups evolved from lessons learned in earlier ver-

CHAPTER 8: UNDERSTANDING AND APPLYING IMPLEMENTATION GROUPS...

sions of the CIS Controls. Previous versions presented all controls as equally important, leading many organizations to struggle with prioritization and resource allocation. Implementing Implementation Groups in Version 7 marked a significant shift toward a more practical, achievable approach to security implementation. This evolution continued in Version 8, with further refinements based on real-world implementation experiences and changing threat landscapes.

The current Implementation Group structure consists of three tiers. **Implementation Group 1 (IG1)** represents basic cyber hygiene, essential for any organization regardless of size or complexity. **Implementation Group 2 (IG2)** builds upon this foundation with more sophisticated controls for organizations with greater resources and needs. **Implementation Group 3 (IG3)** represents the most comprehensive security implementation for organizations requiring advanced security measures.

In modern security programs, Implementation Groups serve multiple crucial roles. They provide a clear starting point for organizations beginning their security journey, offering guidance on prioritizing controls based on available resources. More mature organizations offer a roadmap for the progressive enhancement of security capabilities. This structured approach helps organizations avoid the common pitfall of attempting too quickly, often leading to incomplete or ineffective implementation.

The relationship between Implementation Groups and overall security strategy proves particularly significant. Rather than operating in isolation, Implementation Groups integrate with broader security objectives, risk management processes, and business goals. They help organizations align security investments with risk tolerance and business requirements, ensuring that security measures support rather than hinder organizational objectives.

Implementation Groups also facilitate more effective resource allocation. By clearly defining which controls belong in each group, organizations can better plan their security investments and staffing requirements. This clarity helps security teams justify resource requests and demonstrate clear progression paths for security program development.

Implementation groups make the framework's approach to risk management more practical. Organizations can better understand their security capabilities and identify gaps by comparing their implementations against the appropriate group's requirements. This understanding helps drive more effective risk management decisions and security investments.

Compliance requirements often influence Implementation Group selection. Many regulatory frameworks align with specific control requirements, and understanding these alignments helps organizations choose appropriate Implementation Groups. This alignment helps organizations satisfy compliance requirements while building effective security programs.

Technical architecture considerations are crucial in selecting and implementing the Implementation Group. Different groups may require varying levels of technical sophistication and infrastructure support. Understanding these requirements helps organizations plan their technical evolution alongside their security program development.

CHAPTER 8: UNDERSTANDING AND APPLYING IMPLEMENTATION GROUPS...

Organizational maturity significantly influences the selection and success of the Implementation Group. The groups provide a natural progression path that aligns with increasing organizational security maturity. This alignment helps organizations develop their security capabilities in a structured, sustainable manner.

Implementation Groups also support better communication with stakeholders. They provide a clear framework for discussing security program development with executive leadership, helping justify security investments and demonstrate program progress. This communication aspect proves particularly valuable when seeking support for security initiatives.

The flexibility inherent in Implementation Groups allows organizations to adapt their security programs as needs change. Based on risk assessment and business requirements, organizations can implement higher-group controls in specific areas while maintaining lower-group controls in others. This flexibility helps organizations optimize their security investments while maintaining effective protection.

Success in utilizing Implementation Groups often depends on a realistic assessment of organizational capabilities and needs. **Organizations must carefully evaluate their security posture, available resources, and risk landscape when selecting appropriate Implementation Groups.** This evaluation helps ensure sustainable security program development aligned with organizational capabilities.

Implementation Group 1 (IG1) - Basic Cyber Hygiene

Implementation Group 1 represents the foundation of effective cybersecurity, establishing essential security controls that every organization should implement regardless of size or industry. This basic cyber hygiene level focuses on critical security measures that provide maximum security benefits with minimal resource investment.

Organizations in Implementation Group 1 typically exhibit several common characteristics. **These organizations often operate with limited dedicated IT security resources, relying on small IT teams that handle operational and security responsibilities.** They may have constrained budgets for security investments and limited internal security expertise. However, these organizations still face significant security risks and require effective protection against common cyber threats.

The essential security controls in IG1 focus on fundamental security measures that address the most common attack vectors. **Asset management** forms the cornerstone of IG1 controls, requiring organizations to maintain basic inventories of hardware and software assets. This foundational control enables organizations to understand what they must protect and forms the basis for other security measures.

Configuration management within IG1 emphasizes secure baseline configurations for common systems and applications. Organizations must establish and maintain basic security settings that help prevent common attacks while remaining practical to implement and maintain. This includes fundamental measures like changing default passwords,

CHAPTER 8: UNDERSTANDING AND APPLYING IMPLEMENTATION GROUPS...

disabling unnecessary services, and applying security patches.

Access control in IG1 focuses on basic account management and authentication requirements. Organizations must implement fundamental controls like unique user accounts, basic password policies, and account deactivation procedures. While these controls may seem simple, they prevent many common security incidents when properly implemented.

Resource considerations for IG1 implementation remain practical and achievable. **Organizations typically leverage existing IT staff, supplementing their capabilities with basic security tools and occasional external support.** Many IG1 controls can be implemented using built-in operating system capabilities and free or low-cost security tools, making them accessible even with limited budgets.

Implementation priorities within IG1 focus on addressing the most critical security needs first. Organizations should begin with asset inventory and basic access controls, which provide the foundation for other security measures. Following these foundational controls, organizations can progressively implement additional measures based on risk assessment and resource availability.

Network security in IG1 emphasizes basic protection measures like firewalls and network segmentation. Organizations must implement fundamental network controls that prevent unauthorized access while maintaining necessary business operations. This includes basic network monitoring capabilities to detect and respond to security incidents.

Data protection within IG1 focuses on essential measures to secure sensitive information. Organizations must implement basic controls like data backups and fundamental encryption for sensitive data. While these controls may not provide comprehensive data protection, they address critical data security needs.

Endpoint protection in IG1 emphasizes basic security tools like antivirus software and personal firewalls. Organizations must ensure all devices have fundamental security controls that protect against common malware and network-based attacks. Regular updates and basic monitoring help maintain the effectiveness of these controls.

Common challenges in IG1 implementation often relate to resource constraints and technical complexity. Organizations frequently struggle with maintaining consistent security practices across all systems and users. Limited staff time and expertise can make configuring and maintaining security controls difficult. However, these challenges can be addressed through careful planning and prioritization.

Training and awareness within IG1 focus on basic security practices that all users must understand. Organizations should implement fundamental security awareness training that helps users recognize and respond to common security threats. This training should be practical and relevant to users' daily activities.

Success criteria for IG1 implementation focus on achieving and maintaining basic security capabilities. Organizations should measure success through basic metrics like asset inventory accuracy, patch compliance rates, and incident response effectiveness. Regular assessment helps ensure controls remain effective and identify areas needing improvement.

CHAPTER 8: UNDERSTANDING AND APPLYING IMPLEMENTATION GROUPS...

Documentation requirements for IG1 remain focused on essential procedures and configurations. Organizations should maintain basic documentation of security controls, focusing on information needed for ongoing operations and incident response. While documentation need not be extensive, it should be sufficient to maintain consistency and enable knowledge transfer.

Risk management in IG1 emphasizes understanding and addressing fundamental security risks. Organizations should conduct basic risk assessments that identify critical assets and common threats. This understanding helps guide security investments and control implementation priorities.

Incident response capabilities within IG1 focus on basic preparation and response procedures. Organizations must develop fundamental capabilities to detect and respond to security incidents. While these capabilities may not be sophisticated, they should enable an effective response to common security events.

Success in IG1 implementation often depends on consistently focusing on fundamental security practices while avoiding scope creep into more advanced controls. Organizations should focus on achieving and maintaining basic security hygiene before considering more sophisticated measures.

Implementation Group 2 (IG2) - Intermediate Cyber Hygiene

Implementation Group 2 represents a significant advancement in security maturity, building upon the foundational controls established in IG1. Organizations operating at this level typically manage more complex IT environments and face more sophisticated threats, requiring enhanced security capabilities to maintain effective protection.

Organizations in IG2 commonly demonstrate more mature IT operations with dedicated security resources. These organizations usually maintain separate IT and security teams, though they may not have the extensive specialized security staff in larger enterprises. They often operate in regulated industries or handle sensitive data requiring enhanced protection beyond basic security controls.

The transition from IG1 to IG2 involves a significant expansion of security capabilities. **While IG1 focuses on fundamental security hygiene, IG2 introduces more sophisticated controls to address advanced threats and complex operational requirements.** This expansion requires careful planning to maintain the existing security effectiveness while implementing enhanced capabilities.

Asset management at the IG2 level introduces automated discovery and tracking capabilities. Organizations must implement tools that provide continuous visibility into their IT infrastructure, including dynamic environments like cloud services and virtual systems. This enhanced asset management supports more sophisticated security controls and enables better risk management.

CHAPTER 8: UNDERSTANDING AND APPLYING IMPLEMENTATION GROUPS...

Configuration management becomes more rigorous in IG2, requiring automated configuration assessment and enforcement. Organizations must implement tools that regularly validate system configurations against security baselines and report deviations. This automated approach helps maintain security consistency across larger, more complex environments.

Access control mechanisms in IG2 incorporate more sophisticated authentication and authorization capabilities. Organizations must implement multi-factor authentication for privileged accounts and establish role-based access control systems. These enhanced controls provide stronger protection for sensitive resources while maintaining operational efficiency.

Resource requirements for IG2 implementation increase significantly compared to IG1. Organizations need dedicated security staff and more sophisticated security tools. Budget allocations must support both technology investments and ongoing operational costs. Staff training becomes more critical as security controls become more complex.

The implementation strategy for IG2 requires careful coordination between security and operational teams. Organizations must plan control implementations that enhance security without disrupting business operations. This often involves staged deployments with extensive testing and validation phases.

Network security controls in IG2 expand to include advanced monitoring and protection capabilities. Organizations must implement intrusion detection systems, security information and event management (SIEM) solutions, and enhanced network segmentation. These controls provide deeper visibility into network activities and better threat detection capabilities.

Data protection measures in IG2 include more comprehensive controls like data loss prevention systems and encryption management platforms. Organizations must implement tools that protect sensitive data across various storage locations and transmission paths, including both structured and unstructured data protection capabilities.

Endpoint protection at the IG2 level incorporates advanced threat detection and response capabilities. Organizations must implement endpoint detection and response (EDR) solutions that provide detailed visibility into endpoint activities and enable rapid response to security incidents.

Integration with existing controls requires careful attention to maintain security effectiveness. Organizations must ensure that new IG2 controls enhance rather than conflict with existing IG1 measures. This integration often involves updating procedures and reconfiguring existing tools to work with new security capabilities.

Vulnerability management in IG2 becomes more sophisticated, requiring continuous scanning and risk-based remediation. Organizations must implement automated vulnerability assessment tools and establish processes for prioritizing and tracking remediation efforts. This enhanced approach helps maintain security posture in dynamic environments.

Incident response capabilities expand significantly in IG2. Organizations must establish formal incident response teams and implement automated detection and response capabilities. This includes developing detailed response playbooks and conducting regular incident response exercises.

Success metrics for IG2 implementation focus on technical and operational measures. Organizations should track metrics like vulnerability remediation rates, incident detection times, and control effectiveness measurements. These metrics help demonstrate the security program's value and identify areas for improvement.

Documentation requirements increase substantially in IG2. Organizations must maintain detailed documentation of security architectures, configurations, and procedures. This documentation supports both operational needs and compliance requirements while enabling effective knowledge transfer.

Change management becomes more critical in IG2 environments. Organizations must implement formal change management processes that balance security requirements with operational needs. This includes security impact assessment procedures for proposed changes and implementation validation requirements.

Risk management at the IG2 level requires more sophisticated assessment and treatment capabilities. Organizations must conduct regular risk assessments that consider both technical and business factors. This enhanced risk management approach helps guide security investments and control implementations.

Success in IG2 implementation often depends on maintaining an effective balance between security enhancement and operational efficiency. Organizations must carefully manage resources and priorities to achieve security objectives while supporting business operations.

Implementation Group 3 (IG3) - Advanced Cyber Defense

Implementation Group 3 represents the highest security maturity level within the CIS Controls framework. It encompasses comprehensive security controls designed for organizations facing sophisticated threats or operating in highly regulated environments. These controls provide advanced protection capabilities while requiring significant resources and expertise to implement effectively.

Organizations operating at the IG3 level typically maintain large, complex IT environments with substantial security requirements. These organizations often operate in critical infrastructure sectors, handle highly sensitive data, or face advanced persistent threats. They maintain dedicated security teams with specialized expertise across various security domains and invest significantly in security technology and personnel.

The comprehensive control implementation at the IG3 level extends beyond the enhanced capabilities of IG2, introducing advanced security measures across all control domains. This includes sophisticated threat detection and response capabilities, advanced automation and orchestration, and comprehensive security monitoring across the entire technology infrastructure.

Asset management at the IG3 level incorporates real-time discovery and assessment capabilities. Organizations must continuously monitor their entire technology infrastructure, including ephemeral assets and complex cloud environments. This advanced asset management supports sophisticated security controls and enables proactive risk management.

Configuration management becomes highly automated in IG3, incorporating continuous validation and automated remediation capabilities. Organizations implement sophisticated configuration management platforms that maintain security baselines across diverse technology environments. These platforms automatically detect and correct configuration drift while maintaining detailed audit trails.

Access control mechanisms at the IG3 level implement zero trust principles and advanced authentication technologies. Organizations deploy sophisticated identity and access management platforms that provide granular access control and continuous authentication validation. These systems integrate with various security tools to enable risk-based access decisions.

Advanced resource requirements for IG3 implementation require substantial investment in technology and personnel. Organizations must maintain specialized security teams with expertise in various security domains, including threat hunters, security architects, and incident response specialists. Technology investments encompass enterprise-grade security platforms and advanced monitoring tools.

Sophisticated implementation approaches in IG3 environments require careful orchestration of multiple security technologies and processes. Organizations implement security orchestration and automated response (SOAR) platforms that coordinate various security tools and automate complex response procedures. These implementations require extensive planning and testing to ensure effective operation.

Network security at the IG3 level incorporates advanced threat detection and prevention capabilities. Organizations implement sophisticated network security platforms that provide deep packet inspection, behavioral analysis, and automated threat response. These systems integrate with threat intelligence platforms to enable proactive threat detection and mitigation.

Data protection measures in IG3 environments include advanced encryption management and data governance capabilities. Organizations implement enterprise-grade data protection platforms that provide comprehensive data lifecycle protection, including sophisticated key management systems and automated data classification capabilities.

Endpoint protection at the IG3 level implements advanced endpoint detection and response (EDR) capabilities integrated with network security controls. Organizations deploy sophisticated endpoint security platforms that provide detailed visibility into endpoint activities and enable automated responses to security incidents.

Complex integration requirements in IG3 environments necessitate careful coordination between various security platforms and operational systems. Organizations must implement sophisticated integration architectures that enable effective communication between security tools while maintaining system performance and reliability.

Vulnerability management in IG3 environments incorporates advanced risk assessment and automated remediation capabilities. Organizations implement enterprise vulnerability management platforms that provide continuous assessment and prioritized remediation guidance. These systems integrate with various security tools to enable automated vulnerability remediation.

Incident response capabilities at the IG3 level include sophisticated detection, analysis, and response automation. Organizations maintain dedicated incident response teams supported by advanced security tools. These teams conduct regular exercises and maintain detailed response procedures for various incident types.

Measuring advanced control effectiveness requires sophisticated metrics and assessment capabilities. Organizations implement security analytics platforms that provide detailed insights into security control performance. These platforms enable continuous assessment of security effectiveness and support data-driven security decisions.

The security architecture in IG3 environments requires comprehensive design and regular review. Organizations maintain detailed security architecture documentation that describes control implementations and integration requirements. This architecture undergoes regular review and updates to address emerging threats and changing business requirements.

Change management at the IG3 level implements rigorous control over all system modifications. Organizations maintain sophisticated change management processes, including security impact analysis and automated validation testing. These processes ensure security controls remain effective as systems evolve.

Success in IG3 implementation depends on maintaining effective coordination between various security capabilities while supporting business operations. Organizations must carefully balance advanced security requirements with operational efficiency, ensuring security controls enhance rather than hinder business activities.

Determining Your Implementation Group

Selecting the appropriate Implementation Group is a critical decision influencing an organization's security program. This determination requires careful consideration of multiple factors to ensure the selected Implementation Group aligns with organizational capabilities and security requirements.

Assessment criteria for Implementation Group selection begin with understanding current security capabilities. Organizations must evaluate their existing security controls, technical infrastructure, and operational processes. This evaluation should examine the breadth and depth of current security measures, identifying areas of strength and weakness. The assessment must consider what security controls exist and how effectively they operate within the organization's environment.

Technical infrastructure plays a crucial role in the selection of the Implementation Group. Organizations must evaluate the complexity of their technology environment, including network architecture, system diversity, and operational requirements. Cloud adoption levels significantly influence this assessment, as more complex cloud environments often require more sophisticated security controls. The evaluation should consider current infrastructure and planned technology initiatives that might affect security requirements.

Resource availability fundamentally affects Implementation Group selection. Organizations must realistically assess their security program resources, including both financial and personnel capabilities. This assessment should consider current resources and potential

CHAPTER 8: UNDERSTANDING AND APPLYING IMPLEMENTATION GROUPS...

future investments. The evaluation must examine the quantity of available resources and their quality, including staff expertise and technology effectiveness.

Staff capabilities require particular attention during the implementation group's determination. Organizations must evaluate their security team's size, expertise, and availability. This assessment should consider dedicated security staff and IT personnel supporting security functions. The evaluation must examine current capabilities and the organization's ability to develop or acquire additional security expertise.

Risk assessment considerations significantly influence the selection of the Implementation Group. Organizations must understand their threat landscape, including both current and emerging threats. This assessment should examine potential attack vectors, likely threat actors, and the possible impact of security incidents. The evaluation must consider technical and business risks that could affect the organization.

Industry-specific factors often drive Implementation Group requirements. Organizations must consider their industry's security requirements, including both formal regulations and informal standards. Different industries face varying threat levels and compliance requirements that influence appropriate security controls. The assessment should examine industry-specific security practices and threat patterns.

Data sensitivity plays a crucial role in determining the Implementation Group. Organizations must evaluate the types of data they handle and associated protection requirements. This assessment should consider regulated data like personal information and sensitive business data. The evaluation must examine data volumes, processing requirements, and protection needs.

Business operations significantly impact Implementation Group selection. Organizations must consider how security controls affect their operational capabilities. This assessment should examine business processes, customer requirements, and partner relationships. The evaluation must balance security needs with operational efficiency requirements.

Compliance requirements often influence Implementation Group selection. Organizations must understand their regulatory obligations and associated security control requirements. This assessment should examine both current and anticipated compliance requirements. The evaluation must consider how different Implementation Groups support compliance objectives.

Growth projections affect Implementation Group determination. Organizations must consider how their security needs might evolve as they grow. This assessment should examine planned business initiatives, market expansion plans, and technology evolution. The evaluation must ensure that selected Implementation Groups support current and future security needs.

Partner requirements can influence Implementation Group selection. Organizations must consider security requirements from business partners, customers, or suppliers. This assessment should examine contractual obligations and partner expectations regarding security controls. The evaluation must ensure that selected Implementation Groups satisfy partner security requirements.

CHAPTER 8: UNDERSTANDING AND APPLYING IMPLEMENTATION GROUPS...

Geographic considerations affect Implementation Group determination. Organizations operating across multiple regions must consider varying security requirements and threat landscapes. This assessment should examine both the physical and regulatory implications of geographic distribution. The evaluation must ensure that selected Implementation Groups address security needs across all operating locations.

Integration capabilities influence Implementation Group selection. Organizations must consider how different security controls integrate with existing systems and processes. This assessment should examine technical integration requirements and operational impact. The evaluation must ensure that selected Implementation Groups support effective security integration.

Cost considerations fundamentally affect Implementation Group selection. Organizations must evaluate the implementation and ongoing operational costs associated with different Implementation Groups. This assessment should examine direct costs like technology investments and indirect costs like operational impact. The evaluation must ensure that selected Implementation Groups remain financially sustainable.

Success in selecting an Implementation Group often depends on maintaining realistic expectations while planning for growth. Organizations must choose Implementation Groups that provide appropriate security capabilities while remaining achievable with available resources.

Moving Between Implementation Groups: Strategy and Execution

The transition between Implementation Groups represents a significant evolution in an organization's security program. This progression requires careful planning and systematic execution to ensure security capabilities grow effectively while maintaining operational stability. Understanding how to manage this transition helps organizations enhance security posture while avoiding common implementation challenges.

Growth planning forms the foundation for the successful implementation of Group transitions. Organizations must develop comprehensive plans addressing technical and operational aspects of security program enhancement. This planning begins with a thorough assessment of current security capabilities and a clear definition of target state requirements. The growth plan must consider various factors, including technology infrastructure, staff capabilities, and operational processes that support security controls.

Progression strategy development requires careful consideration of implementation sequence and timing. Organizations must determine which additional controls to implement first based on factors like risk reduction potential and implementation complexity. This strategic approach helps organizations maintain security effectiveness during transition while optimizing resource utilization. The progression strategy should include clear milestones that help track implementation progress and validate security improvements.

Resource planning plays a crucial role in successful transitions.

Organizations must identify and allocate necessary resources before implementing additional controls. This includes financial resources for technology investments and personnel resources for implementation and ongoing operations. Resource planning must consider both immediate implementation needs and long-term operational requirements to ensure sustainable security enhancement.

Technical skill development requires particular attention during transitions. Organizations must assess current staff capabilities and identify additional skills for implementing new controls. This assessment should lead to structured training programs that prepare staff for new security responsibilities. The skill development plan must balance immediate training needs with ongoing professional development requirements.

Change management becomes increasingly important as organizations implement more sophisticated controls. Organizations must establish effective processes for managing security changes while maintaining operational stability. This includes clear communication procedures, stakeholder engagement strategies, and impact assessment methodologies. Change management processes should scale with increasing control complexity to ensure effective implementation.

Risk considerations significantly influence transition planning and execution. Organizations must regularly assess how security changes affect their risk posture and adjust implementation plans accordingly. This includes evaluating both security improvements and potential risks introduced during transition periods. Risk assessment should remain continuous throughout the transition to ensure security enhancements effectively address organizational risks.

Implementation sequencing requires careful planning to maintain security effectiveness. Organizations must determine logical progression paths that build upon existing controls while introducing new capabilities. This sequencing should consider dependencies between different controls and their implementation requirements. The implementation sequence must maintain basic security effectiveness while progressively enhancing security capabilities.

Documentation requirements increase as organizations move to higher Implementation Groups. Organizations must enhance security documentation to support more sophisticated controls and complex operational procedures. This documentation evolution should maintain clarity while providing necessary detail for advanced security operations. Documentation updates should remain ongoing throughout the transition process.

Metrics and measurement capabilities must evolve during transitions. Organizations must develop more sophisticated methods for measuring security effectiveness as they implement advanced controls. This includes technical metrics for specific controls and broader measurements of security program effectiveness. Measurement capabilities should grow alongside security control sophistication.

Integration planning becomes more critical with advanced implementations. Organizations must carefully plan how new security controls integrate with existing systems and processes. This integration planning should address both technical and operational aspects of security enhancement. Integration requirements often influence implementation timing and resource allocation decisions.

Operational impact requires careful consideration during transitions.

CHAPTER 8: UNDERSTANDING AND APPLYING IMPLEMENTATION GROUPS...

Organizations must assess how new security controls affect business operations and plan accordingly. This includes evaluating potential disruptions and developing mitigation strategies. Operational impact assessment should influence implementation scheduling and change management approaches.

The definition of success criteria helps guide transition efforts effectively. Organizations must establish clear metrics for measuring implementation success at each stage of their progression. These criteria should address both technical implementation effectiveness and operational impact. Success measurements help validate security improvements and identify areas needing adjustment.

Stakeholder management becomes increasingly important during transitions. Organizations must maintain effective communication with various stakeholders throughout the implementation process. This includes informing leadership of progress and ensuring users understand new security requirements. Stakeholder engagement helps maintain support for security enhancements while managing expectations.

Compliance validation remains essential during transitions. Organizations must ensure new security implementations maintain compliance with relevant requirements. This includes validating that enhanced controls meet both current and anticipated compliance needs. Compliance considerations often influence implementation priorities and approaches.

Budget management requires particular attention during transitions. Organizations must carefully track and manage costs associated with implementing new controls, including both direct implementation costs and ongoing operational expenses. Budget management helps ensure security enhancements remain financially sustainable while delivering expected benefits.

Success transitioning between Implementation Groups often depends on balancing advancement and stability. Organizations must enhance their security capabilities while ensuring existing controls remain effective throughout the transition process.

Implementation Group Best Practices

Best practices for implementing CIS Controls across different Implementation Groups emerge from collective experience across numerous organizations. Understanding these practices helps organizations avoid common implementation challenges while optimizing their security investments.

Implementation Group 1's starting points focus on establishing fundamental security controls. Organizations should begin with asset inventory and basic security configurations, as these controls provide the foundation for other security measures. Initial implementation should emphasize controls that provide immediate risk reduction with minimal resource requirements. Basic account management and access control measures typically follow asset management implementation.

Implementation Group 2 starting points build upon established IG1 controls. Organizations should begin their IG2 implementation by enhancing existing controls with more sophisticated capabilities.

CHAPTER 8: UNDERSTANDING AND APPLYING IMPLEMENTATION GROUPS...

The initial focus typically involves implementing automated security assessment tools and enhanced monitoring capabilities. These enhancements should maintain existing security effectiveness while introducing more advanced protection measures.

Implementation Group 3 implementations begin with a comprehensive security program assessment. Before beginning IG3 implementation, organizations should evaluate their existing security capabilities against advanced control requirements. The initial focus typically involves implementing advanced security architectures and sophisticated monitoring capabilities. These implementations require careful planning to maintain operational stability.

Common pitfalls often emerge during implementation efforts. Organizations frequently attempt to implement too many controls simultaneously, leading to incomplete or ineffective implementations. Another common mistake involves inadequate resource allocation, particularly underestimating ongoing operational requirements. Implementation planning should explicitly address these potential issues.

Resource allocation requires careful consideration across all Implementation Groups. Organizations must allocate sufficient resources not only for initial implementation but also for ongoing operations and maintenance. Resource planning should consider direct costs like technology investments and indirect costs like staff time and training requirements. Effective resource allocation helps ensure sustainable security improvements.

Team structure significantly influences implementation success. Organizations should establish clear roles and responsibilities for security implementation and operations. Team structures should align with Implementation Group requirements and organizational capabilities. IG1 implementations might rely on general IT staff, while IG2 and IG3 typically require dedicated security personnel.

Documentation requirements vary across Implementation Groups but remain essential for all implementations. Organizations should maintain comprehensive documentation of their security controls, including implementation details and operational procedures. Documentation should scale with implementation complexity, providing appropriate detail for each control level. Regular documentation updates help maintain program effectiveness.

Measurement and metrics become increasingly sophisticated across Implementation Groups. Organizations should establish appropriate metrics for measuring both implementation progress and control effectiveness. IG1 metrics might focus on basic coverage and compliance, while IG2 and IG3 require more sophisticated effectiveness measurements. Metrics should provide meaningful insight into security program performance.

Implementation planning requires particular attention to prerequisite requirements. Organizations must identify and address dependencies between different controls before beginning implementation. This includes both technical prerequisites like infrastructure requirements and operational prerequisites like staff training. Proper prerequisite planning helps prevent implementation delays.

Change management practices should align with the Implementation Group's complexity. Organizations implementing IG1 controls might use basic change management processes, while IG2 and IG3 implementations require more rigorous procedures. Change management

CHAPTER 8: UNDERSTANDING AND APPLYING IMPLEMENTATION GROUPS...

should balance security requirements with operational needs. Effective change management helps maintain stability during implementation.

Testing requirements increase with Implementation Group sophistication. Organizations should establish appropriate testing procedures for validating control implementations. Testing should verify both technical effectiveness and operational impact. Regular testing helps ensure controls operate effectively and identify potential issues early.

Communication strategies significantly influence implementation success. Organizations should maintain clear communication with stakeholders throughout implementation efforts. Communication should address technical details for implementation teams and the business impact on leadership. Effective communication helps maintain support for security initiatives.

Integration planning becomes more critical in higher Implementation Groups. Organizations must carefully plan how new controls integrate with existing systems and processes. Integration planning should address both technical and operational aspects of control implementation. Proper integration helps maintain operational efficiency while enhancing security.

The definition of success criteria helps guide implementation efforts effectively. Organizations should establish clear metrics for measuring implementation success at each stage. Success criteria should address both technical effectiveness and business alignment. Regular assessment against success criteria helps validate implementation progress.

Training requirements vary across Implementation Groups but remain essential for all implementations. Organizations should provide appropriate training for staff implementing and operating security controls, aligning with Implementation Group requirements and staff responsibilities. Ongoing training helps maintain security program effectiveness.

Best practices evolve continuously as organizations gain experience in implementation. Regular review and refinement of implementation practices help organizations optimize their security programs. Sharing implementation experiences within security communities contributes to collective knowledge improvement.

Implementation Group Case Studies and Real-World Examples

Real-world implementations of CIS Controls provide valuable insights into effective security program development. These case studies demonstrate practical approaches to implementing controls across different organizational contexts while highlighting key lessons learned from actual implementations.

A mid-sized manufacturing organization demonstrates effective IG1 implementation. Beginning with limited security controls, this organization focused initially on implementing fundamental asset management capabilities. They deployed basic asset discovery tools and established manual processes for tracking system inventory. This foundation enabled them to identify unauthorized systems and maintain basic security oversight. Following asset management implementation, they established basic security configurations for common

CHAPTER 8: UNDERSTANDING AND APPLYING IMPLEMENTATION GROUPS...

systems, significantly reducing their attack surface. Their measured approach to implementation helped them achieve sustainable security improvements while maintaining operational efficiency.

The manufacturing organization's experience highlighted several key implementation factors. Their focus on fundamental controls before attempting more advanced measures helped them build sustainable security capabilities. Maintaining clear documentation of their implementation process enabled effective knowledge transfer as their security program matured. Their success demonstrates the value of thorough planning and systematic implementation approaches.

A regional healthcare provider illustrates the successful transition from IG1 to IG2. Having established basic security controls, they recognized the need for enhanced security capabilities to protect sensitive patient data. Their transition began with a careful assessment of existing controls and the identification of necessary enhancements. During the transition period, they implemented automated security assessment tools while maintaining existing manual processes. This parallel operation helped ensure continuous security coverage during their enhancement efforts.

The healthcare provider's transition experience reveals important considerations for security program enhancement. Their phased approach to implementing new capabilities helped maintain operational stability throughout the transition. Focusing on staff training alongside technical implementations ensured their team could effectively operate enhanced security controls. Their experience demonstrates the importance of balanced attention to security enhancement's technical and operational aspects.

A financial services organization exemplifies successful IG3 implementation. Operating in a highly regulated environment with sophisticated threat actors, this organization implemented comprehensive security controls across its environment. It established advanced security monitoring capabilities integrated with automated response systems. Its implementation included sophisticated threat-hunting capabilities and advanced analytics for detecting subtle attack patterns. Its success required substantial investment in both technology and personnel.

The financial organization's implementation highlights crucial factors for advanced security programs. Their emphasis on integration between different security controls helped maximize effectiveness while optimizing resource utilization. Maintaining comprehensive documentation of their security architecture and operational procedures enabled consistent security operations across their environment. Their experience demonstrates the importance of systematic approaches to complex security implementations.

Common lessons emerge across these implementations. Organizations successful in implementing CIS Controls typically maintain a strong focus on foundational security measures while progressively enhancing their capabilities. They recognize the importance of proper resource allocation and staff development in supporting security improvements. Their documentation practices enable knowledge transfer and consistent operations.

Successful implementations consistently demonstrate the value of proper planning. Organizations that carefully assess their current capabilities before implementation typically achieve better results. Their planning addresses both technical requirements and operational considerations. This comprehensive approach helps ensure sustainable security improvements.

Staff development proves crucial across all implementation levels. Organizations that invest in training and skill development typically implement controls more effectively. Their staff training aligns with implementation requirements and security program objectives. This alignment helps maintain security program effectiveness as capabilities expand.

Documentation practices significantly influence implementation success. Organizations that maintain comprehensive documentation of their security controls typically achieve better operational consistency. Their documentation supports both daily operations and security program enhancement. Proper documentation also helps maintain security effectiveness during staff changes.

Integration requirements receive careful attention in successful implementations. Organizations effectively integrating new security controls with existing systems typically maintain better operational efficiency. Their integration planning addresses both technical and procedural aspects of security enhancement. This comprehensive approach helps prevent operational disruptions during implementation.

Measurement practices evolve with security program maturity. Organizations implementing more sophisticated controls typically develop enhanced measurement capabilities. Their metrics provide meaningful insight into security program effectiveness. Regular measurement helps validate security improvements and identify enhancement opportunities.

Change management practices significantly influence implementation success. Organizations maintaining effective change management processes typically implement controls more smoothly. Their procedures balance security requirements with operational needs. This balanced approach helps maintain stability during security enhancement.

Resource allocation remains crucial across all implementation levels. Organizations that properly allocate resources for both implementation and operations typically achieve better results. Their resource planning addresses ongoing operational requirements alongside implementation needs. This comprehensive planning helps ensure sustainable security improvements.

Success stories consistently demonstrate the value of systematic approaches to security implementation. Organizations following structured implementation methodologies typically achieve better results. Their systematic approaches help ensure comprehensive security coverage while optimizing resource utilization.

Chapter 9: Maintaining and Enhancing Your Cybersecurity Posture

Routine Assessments and Audits: Maintaining Security Effectiveness

Regular assessment and audit processes are the foundation for maintaining an effective security program. While many organizations conduct periodic evaluations, the key to success lies in developing a structured, ongoing approach that provides continuous visibility into security posture while supporting continuous improvement efforts.

The effectiveness of security assessments depends heavily on establishing proper foundations. A technology company discovered this when it attempted to implement quarterly security reviews without first defining clear evaluation criteria. Their initial assessments produced inconsistent results that couldn't be effectively compared over time. Success came only after it developed standardized evaluation criteria aligned with its security objectives and compliance requirements.

A comprehensive assessment program must address multiple as-

pects of security controls. A financial services organization initially focused solely on technical control testing, missing important processes and procedural gaps. After expanding its assessment scope to include process evaluation, documentation review, and effectiveness measurement, it achieved better results, providing a more complete view of its security posture.

Assessment frequency requires careful consideration of both security needs and operational constraints. A healthcare provider initially attempted monthly comprehensive assessments of all security controls, quickly overwhelming their security team. They succeeded after implementing a tiered approach where critical controls underwent frequent automated assessment while comprehensive manual reviews occurred quarterly, creating a sustainable rhythm for their security team.

Documentation plays a crucial role in assessment effectiveness. A manufacturing company struggled to demonstrate security improvements until they implemented structured documentation practices that captured assessment findings, remediation efforts, and validation results. This documentation satisfied audit requirements and provided valuable insights for security program enhancement.

Automation proves essential for sustainable assessment programs. A retail organization initially relied on manual assessment processes, leading to inconsistent execution and delayed reporting. Their program improved significantly after implementing automated assessment tools that provided continuous control validation while freeing security team resources for more complex evaluation tasks.

The relationship between assessments and audits requires careful

management. A technology services provider initially treated these as separate activities, creating duplicate efforts and conflicting findings. They achieved better results after aligning their assessment program with audit requirements, using regular assessments to maintain continuous compliance readiness.

Assessment criteria must evolve with changing security requirements. A financial institution discovered this when its static assessment criteria failed to address emerging threats and new compliance requirements. It improved its program by implementing regular criteria reviews and updates, ensuring its assessments remained relevant and effective.

Management support proves crucial for assessment program success. A healthcare organization struggled with assessment effectiveness until they secured executive sponsorship that ensured proper resource allocation and organizational priority. This support helped them maintain program momentum and drive security improvements based on assessment findings.

Integration with existing processes enhances assessment effectiveness. A manufacturing firm initially operated its assessment program in isolation, limiting its impact on security improvements. However, it became more effective after integrating with change management, incident response, and risk management processes, creating a coordinated approach to security enhancement.

Skills development requires ongoing attention. A technology company found that its assessment quality suffered due to knowledge gaps in its security team. They improved results through targeted training programs that enhanced their team's ability to conduct effective assessments and interpret findings accurately.

Metrics and reporting deserve careful consideration. A financial services provider struggled to demonstrate assessment value due to overly technical reporting that failed to resonate with business stakeholders. They achieved better results after developing business-aligned metrics and clear reporting formats that effectively communicated security status and improvement needs.

Tools selection impacts assessment sustainability. A healthcare organization initially chose complex assessment tools that required significant expertise to operate effectively. They achieved better results after selecting tools that balanced comprehensive capabilities with usability, enabling broader team participation in assessment activities.

Communication strategies significantly influence assessment effectiveness. A retail company improved its program by developing clear communication channels between assessment teams and system owners, facilitating better cooperation and more effective remediation efforts.

External perspective helps maintain assessment objectivity. A technology services provider enhanced their program by periodically incorporating third-party assessments that provided fresh perspectives and validated their internal findings.

Success in maintaining effective assessment programs often depends on finding the right balance between thoroughness and practicality. Organizations that maintain this balance while continuously refining their approach based on operational experience typically achieve better security outcomes.

Adapting to New Threats: Maintaining Security Effectiveness in a Dynamic Landscape

Adapting to evolving threats represents one of the most critical aspects of maintaining an effective security program. Organizations must develop systematic approaches for identifying, analyzing, and responding to new threats while maintaining existing security controls. This dynamic balance between current protection and future preparation determines long-term security effectiveness.

Threat intelligence integration forms the foundation of adaptive security capabilities. A financial services organization discovered this when it failed to detect a series of emerging attack patterns targeting its industry. Its security posture improved significantly after implementing a structured threat intelligence program that combined commercial feeds with industry-specific information sharing. This comprehensive approach helped it identify and prepare for new threats before they materialized in its environment.

Technical adaptability requires careful architectural design. A healthcare provider initially struggled implementing new security controls due to rigid infrastructure design. They achieved better results after adopting a modular security architecture that allowed rapid deployment of new controls and quick adaptation of existing defenses. This flexibility proved crucial when responding to zero-day vulnerabilities that required immediate control adjustments.

Process adaptation deserves equal attention to technical changes. A manufacturing company found its incident response processes inadequate when facing new attack techniques. Their effectiveness improved after implementing adaptive response procedures that could quickly incorporate new threat information and adjust response strategies accordingly. This procedural flexibility helped them maintain effective response capabilities as threats evolved.

Security tool selection significantly impacts adaptation capabilities. A technology company initially chose security tools that provided strong current protection but limited flexibility for addressing new threats. They enhanced their adaptive capabilities by selecting tools that offered current protection and extensibility for addressing emerging threats. This balanced approach helped them maintain current security while preparing for future challenges.

Training programs require continuous updates to address new threats. A retail organization discovered that its security awareness program failed to address emerging social engineering techniques targeting its industry. It improved its preparedness by implementing dynamic training content that incorporated recent threat information and attack examples, helping its staff recognize and respond to new attack patterns.

Automation plays a crucial role in threat adaptation. A financial institution initially relied on manual processes for implementing new security controls, leading to delayed responses to emerging threats. Their adaptation capabilities improved significantly after implementing automation frameworks that enabled rapid deployment of new controls and quick adjustment of existing defenses.

Testing capabilities must evolve with threats. A healthcare organization found that its security testing failed to identify vulnerabilities exploited by new attack techniques. It enhanced its security validation by implementing adaptive testing procedures that incorporated emerging threat information into its assessment methodology. This approach helped it identify and address security gaps before they could be exploited.

Information sharing enhances adaptive capabilities. A manufacturing firm improved its threat response by actively participating in industry information-sharing groups that provided early warning of new attacks targeting its sector. This collaborative approach helped them prepare for emerging threats while sharing their experiences to benefit others.

Risk assessment processes need regular updates to address new threats. A technology services provider enhanced their security program by implementing dynamic risk assessment procedures that could quickly incorporate new threat information and adjust risk calculations accordingly. This adaptive approach helped them maintain accurate risk visibility as the threat landscape evolved.

Incident response capabilities require continuous enhancement. A financial services organization improved its security posture by developing flexible incident response procedures that could adapt to new attack patterns. Their approach included regular updates to response playbooks based on emerging threat information and lessons learned from actual incidents.

Change management processes impact adaptation effectiveness. A healthcare provider enhanced their security program by implementing flexible change management procedures that could expedite security updates in response to critical threats while maintaining necessary control over system modifications. This balanced approach helped them respond quickly to new threats without compromising operational stability.

Documentation practices need to support rapid adaptation. A manufacturing company improved its security program by implementing dynamic documentation processes that could quickly incorporate new threat information and control modifications. This approach helped them maintain accurate security documentation while supporting rapid response to emerging threats.

Measurement systems must evolve to track new threats. A technology company enhanced its security program by implementing adaptive metrics that could incorporate new threat indicators and adjust measurement criteria accordingly. This dynamic approach helped them maintain meaningful security measurements as threats evolved.

Budget planning needs to account for emerging threats. A retail organization improved its security posture by implementing flexible budget allocation processes that maintained reserves for addressing unexpected threats. This financial flexibility helped them respond effectively to emerging security challenges without disrupting planned security improvements.

Success in adapting to new threats often depends on maintaining the balance between current security needs and future preparation. Organizations that achieve this balance while continuously refining their adaptive capabilities typically achieve better security outcomes over time.

Leveraging Community Knowledge and Resources: Harnessing Collective Security Intelligence

The cybersecurity community represents an invaluable resource for organizations seeking to enhance their security posture. Successfully leveraging this collective knowledge requires structured approaches for engagement, information sharing, and practical implementation of community insights. Understanding how to tap into and utilize these resources effectively can significantly enhance an organization's security capabilities.

Information-sharing communities play a crucial role in modern security programs. A financial services organization discovered this when they detected an emerging attack pattern that seemed unique to their environment. Upon engaging with their sector's Information Sharing and Analysis Center (ISAC), they discovered other institutions experiencing similar attacks. This community engagement helped them develop more effective countermeasures based on collective experience rather than facing a threat in isolation.

Technical communities provide essential insights for security implementation. A healthcare provider significantly improved its security controls after participating in technical forums focused on implementing CIS Controls in healthcare environments. Other organizations' practical experiences helped them avoid common implementation pitfalls and adopt proven approaches for their specific operational context.

Open-source intelligence communities offer valuable threat awareness resources. A manufacturing company enhanced its threat detection capabilities by actively participating in open-source threat intelligence sharing platforms. This engagement provided early warning of emerging threats and access to community-developed detection rules, which improved its security monitoring effectiveness.

Professional associations provide structured knowledge-sharing opportunities. A technology company improved its security program by engaging with professional organizations that offered specialized training, certification programs, and peer networking opportunities. This formal engagement helped them stay current with evolving security practices while building valuable professional relationships.

Security research communities contribute critical insights into emerging threats. A retail organization strengthened its defense capabilities by following security research publications and participating in research-focused forums. This engagement helped them understand emerging attack techniques and develop proactive defense strategies based on cutting-edge research.

Vendor communities often provide valuable implementation expertise. A financial institution improved its security tool effectiveness by actively participating in vendor-sponsored user communities. These forums provided access to implementation best practices, configuration guidance, and practical solutions to common challenges encountered with specific security tools.

Local security groups offer unique networking and knowledge-sharing opportunities. A healthcare organization enhanced its security program by participating in regional security meetups and conferences. These local connections provided valuable insights into area-specific threats and opportunities for direct collaboration with nearby organizations facing similar challenges.

Public-private partnerships facilitate important information exchange. A manufacturing firm strengthened its security posture by participating in government-sponsored information-sharing programs. This engagement provided access to threat intelligence and security guidance not readily available through other channels.

Academic partnerships can provide access to emerging security research. A technology services provider improved their security capabilities by establishing relationships with university cybersecurity programs. These partnerships provided access to cutting-edge research and opportunities to influence security research directions relevant to their operational needs.

Industry working groups contribute to standards development and best practices. A financial services organization enhanced its security program by participating in industry groups focused on developing security standards and implementation guidance. This engagement helped them influence industry standards while gaining early insight into emerging security practices.

Online security communities provide rapid access to collective problem-solving resources. A healthcare provider improved their incident response capabilities by engaging with online security communities that offered real-time assistance during security incidents. This community support helped them resolve complex security challenges more effectively than in isolation.

Security conferences offer concentrated learning and networking opportunities. A manufacturing company enhanced its security knowledge by regularly attending industry conferences. These events provided access to comprehensive security updates, hands-on training opportunities, and valuable peer networking.

Bug bounty communities help identify security vulnerabilities. A technology company improved its application security by engaging with bug bounty platforms that connected it with security researchers. This community engagement helped it identify and address security vulnerabilities before they could be exploited maliciously.

Code-sharing communities provide access to security tools and scripts. A retail organization enhanced its security automation capabilities by participating in code-sharing platforms focused on security tools. This engagement provided access to community-developed security tools and opportunities to contribute their own solutions to the community.

Success in leveraging community knowledge often depends on active engagement while contributing to the community. Organizations that balance consumption and contribution typically benefit most from community resources while helping advance collective security knowledge.

Chapter 10: Navigating Implementation Challenges

Common Implementation Pitfalls and Their Solutions: A Practical Guide

Implementing CIS Controls often presents organizations with significant challenges that can derail security improvements when not properly addressed. Understanding common implementation pitfalls and their solutions helps organizations navigate these challenges more effectively while maintaining steady progress toward their security objectives.

Scope management frequently emerges as an early challenge. A financial services organization initially attempted to implement all CIS Controls simultaneously across its entire infrastructure. This ambitious approach quickly overwhelmed their security team and led to incomplete implementations across multiple controls. Their implementation succeeded only after adopting a phased approach that prioritized critical systems and fundamental controls before expanding to broader coverage. This measured approach allowed them to build momentum through early successes while developing implementation expertise.

Resource allocation presents another significant challenge. A healthcare provider struggled with implementation progress when they underestimated the staff time required for proper control deployment. Their program improved after developing detailed resource planning for implementation and ongoing maintenance requirements. This comprehensive planning helped them maintain consistent progress while avoiding staff burnout.

Technical prerequisites often create unexpected roadblocks. A manufacturing company discovered its aging infrastructure couldn't support several critical security controls, forcing implementation delays while it upgraded core systems. They succeeded by incorporating infrastructure assessment into their planning phase, identifying and addressing technical dependencies before beginning control implementation. This proactive approach helped them avoid similar surprises in subsequent implementation phases.

Documentation gaps frequently hinder implementation efforts. A technology company struggled to maintain consistent control implementation across different teams due to inadequate documentation. Their program improved significantly after developing comprehensive implementation guides that detailed specific steps, configuration requirements, and validation procedures. This documentation investment helped them maintain implementation quality while reducing reliance on key personnel.

Integration challenges often emerge when implementing new controls. A retail organization encountered significant disruption when new security controls conflicted with existing business applications.

CHAPTER 10: NAVIGATING IMPLEMENTATION CHALLENGES

They achieved better results after implementing a thorough testing process that validated control compatibility before production deployment. This validation approach helped them maintain business operations while improving security.

Stakeholder resistance can significantly impact implementation success. A financial institution faced persistent delays when business units resisted security changes that affected their workflows. Their implementation succeeded after developing a stakeholder engagement strategy that incorporated business input into control implementation planning. This collaborative approach helped them maintain implementation momentum while addressing legitimate business concerns.

Compliance alignment often creates implementation complexity. A healthcare organization struggled to align CIS Control implementation with various regulatory requirements. Their program improved after developing compliance mapping that showed how to control implementation and satisfied multiple regulatory frameworks. This integrated approach helped them optimize their implementation effort while maintaining compliance.

Change management frequently presents significant challenges. A manufacturing firm encountered resistance when security changes disrupted established work patterns. They achieved better results after implementing a comprehensive change management process that included clear communication, user training, and phased deployments. This structured approach helped them implement controls while minimizing operational disruption.

Technology selection can create long-term challenges. A technology company initially chose security tools based primarily on current requirements, later discovering these tools couldn't scale to meet growing needs. Their implementation improved after developing selection criteria that considered current requirements and future scalability. This forward-looking approach helped them avoid costly tool replacements.

Skill gaps often impede implementation progress. A retail organization found that its security team lacked the expertise needed for advanced control implementation. Their program succeeded after developing a skills development program that aligned training with implementation requirements. This investment in team capabilities helped them maintain implementation quality while reducing dependence on external expertise.

Monitoring and measurement challenges frequently emerge. A financial services provider struggled to demonstrate implementation effectiveness due to inadequate success metrics. Their program improved after developing specific metrics measuring implementation progress and control effectiveness. This measurement framework helped them validate security improvements while identifying areas needing attention.

Process integration often presents unexpected challenges. A healthcare provider encountered difficulties when new security controls conflicted with existing IT processes. They achieved better results after conducting process impact analysis before implementing new controls. This analytical approach helped them identify and address process conflicts early.

Budget management frequently creates implementation challenges. A manufacturing company struggled with implementation when

CHAPTER 10: NAVIGATING IMPLEMENTATION CHALLENGES

security projects exceeded initial cost estimates. Their program improved after developing comprehensive budgeting that included direct costs and operational impacts. This financial planning helped them maintain steady implementation progress while avoiding budget surprises.

Communication gaps often hinder implementation success. A technology services provider improved implementation by establishing clear communication channels between security teams and system owners. This enhanced communication helped them address implementation challenges more effectively while maintaining stakeholder support.

Success in avoiding implementation pitfalls often depends on balancing thoroughness and practicality. Organizations that combine careful planning with flexibility to address emerging challenges typically achieve better implementation outcomes.

Securing Executive Support and Funding: Building Leadership Commitment to Security

Securing executive support and funding for CIS Controls implementation represents a critical success factor many organizations struggle to achieve. The ability to effectively communicate security needs and justify investments in business terms often determines whether security initiatives receive necessary resources and organizational priority.

Executive engagement begins with understanding business prior-

ities. A financial services organization initially struggled to secure funding when it presented its security program purely in technical terms. However, its approach succeeded after aligning its security initiatives with specific business objectives and risk management goals. This business-focused presentation helped executives understand how security investments supported organizational success.

Risk quantification plays a crucial role in securing executive support. A healthcare provider gained significant funding after developing a risk-based justification that quantified potential losses from security incidents. By comparing these potential losses with proposed security investments, they helped executives understand the return on security investment in business terms. This quantitative approach proved particularly effective in budget discussions.

Regulatory compliance often provides compelling justification for security investments. A manufacturing company secured executive support by demonstrating how CIS Controls implementation would address multiple regulatory requirements simultaneously. This compliance-focused approach resonated with leadership concerned about regulatory risks and audit findings. Their presentation showed how strategic security investments could reduce compliance costs while improving overall security posture.

Industry comparisons can effectively influence executive decisions. A technology company gained leadership support by presenting security benchmark data showing that its security investments lagged behind industry peers. This competitive analysis helped executives understand how security investments relate to market position and customer trust. The comparison provided concrete justification for increasing security funding to maintain market competitiveness.

Project structuring significantly impacts executive support. A retail organization improved funding success by breaking its security program into discrete projects with clear deliverables and measurable outcomes. This structured approach helped executives understand specific investment requirements and expected returns. The clarity helped build confidence in the security team's ability to deliver value from investments.

Performance metrics prove essential for maintaining executive support. A financial institution sustained long-term funding by developing executive-level security metrics demonstrating program effectiveness. These metrics focused on business impacts rather than technical details, helping executives understand the value delivered by security investments. Regular metric reviews kept security visible at the executive level.

Cost optimization demonstrates financial stewardship. A healthcare organization strengthened executive support by showing how its security program optimized existing investments while strategically adding new capabilities. This efficiency-focused approach demonstrated responsible resource management, building executive confidence in security spending requests. Their presentation highlighted cost savings from integrated security solutions.

Incident examples often provide compelling justification. A manufacturing firm secured increased funding after presenting a detailed analysis of how recent industry incidents could impact their organization. This analysis included specific cost estimates and business impact scenarios, helping executives understand security risks concretely. The real-world examples made security risks more tangible for leadership.

Strategic alignment enhances executive engagement. A technology services provider gained sustained support by showing how their security program supported key business initiatives. This alignment helped executives see security as an enabler of business success rather than just a cost center. Their presentation demonstrated how security investments facilitated business growth and innovation.

Communication style significantly influences executive response. A retail company improved executive engagement by adapting its security communications to executive preferences. They replaced technical details with business impacts and strategic implications, making security discussions more relevant for leadership. This tailored communication approach helped maintain executive attention and support.

Project governance helps maintain executive confidence. A financial services organization sustained support by implementing clear governance structures for security initiatives. Regular executive updates focused on progress, challenges, and business impacts rather than technical details. This governance approach kept executives appropriately informed while demonstrating professional program management.

Budget planning requires a strategic approach. A healthcare provider secured consistent funding by developing multi-year security investment plans aligned with business planning cycles. This strategic planning helped executives understand and incorporate long-term security requirements into business planning. The forward-looking approach prevented funding surprises.

Success metrics must resonate with executives. A manufacturing company maintained support by developing success metrics that directly linked security improvements to business objectives. These metrics helped executives understand security program value in business terms, sustaining support for ongoing investments. Regular metric reviews kept security achievements visible to leadership.

Relationship building plays a crucial role in executive support. A technology company strengthened security funding by developing strong relationships between security leadership and executives. Regular informal discussions helped executives understand security challenges and opportunities, building trust in the security team's judgment. These relationships proved valuable during critical funding decisions.

Success in securing executive support often depends on maintaining consistent business focus while demonstrating clear value from security investments. Organizations that effectively communicate security value in business terms typically achieve better support for their security programs.

Chapter 11: Future-Proofing Your Cybersecurity with CIS Controls

Adapting CIS Controls to Emerging Technologies and Trends

The rapid evolution of technology landscapes continuously challenges traditional approaches to implementing CIS Controls. Adapting these controls effectively requires understanding fundamental security principles and how they apply to emerging technologies. This adaptation process must balance maintaining security effectiveness while supporting technological innovation.

Cloud-native architectures fundamentally change how organizations must implement security controls. Traditional asset management, configuration control, and security monitoring approaches require significant adaptation to the cloud environment. The dynamic nature of cloud resources demands more automated, API-driven approaches to security control implementation.

Container technologies introduce new complexities in security control implementation. The ephemeral nature of containers challenges traditional security monitoring and control approaches. Effective container security requires adapting controls to operate at both the container and orchestration levels while maintaining visibility into rapidly changing environments.

Zero-trust architectures represent a paradigm shift in security control implementation. Rather than focusing primarily on perimeter security, controls must adapt to support continuous authentication and authorization throughout the infrastructure. This shift requires fundamental changes in how organizations implement access controls and monitor security status.

Internet of Things (IoT) devices present unique challenges that require adapting traditional security controls. Limited device capabilities, diverse communication protocols, and scale of deployment necessitate new approaches to security control implementation. Network segmentation and behavior-based monitoring become increasingly important in IoT environments.

Edge computing shifts security control requirements from centralized to distributed models. Traditional centralized security approaches must adapt to operate effectively at edge locations while maintaining security visibility and management. This adaptation requires balancing local processing requirements with centralized control needs.

Artificial Intelligence and Machine Learning systems introduce new security considerations that existing controls must address. Protecting AI/ML systems requires adapting controls to address unique risks like data poisoning and model integrity. Security controls must evolve to protect the AI systems and the data they process.

5G networks create opportunities and challenges for security control implementation. Their increased speed and capacity require adapted approaches to security monitoring and control. Network slicing capabilities introduce new security considerations that controls must address.

Quantum computing impacts require forward-looking adaptation of security controls, particularly in cryptographic areas. Organizations must begin preparing for quantum computing threats by adapting their cryptographic controls and maintaining flexibility to implement quantum-resistant solutions as they emerge.

DevOps practices necessitate integrating security controls directly into development and deployment pipelines. Traditional security control approaches must adapt to operate within automated CI/CD workflows while maintaining effectiveness. This integration requires rethinking how security controls are implemented and validated.

Microservices architectures demand new approaches to security control implementation. Their distributed nature requires adapting traditional security controls to operate effectively across service boundaries while maintaining an overall security posture.

Serverless computing challenges traditional approaches to security control implementation. The abstracted nature of serverless environments requires adapting controls to operate effectively without direct access to the underlying infrastructure. This adaptation demands new approaches to security monitoring and control.

Multi-cloud environments require adapting controls to operate consistently across different cloud providers. Security controls must evolve to provide unified protection across diverse cloud environments while accommodating provider-specific characteristics.

Augmented and virtual reality systems introduce novel security considerations that existing controls must address. Protecting mixed reality environments requires adapting controls to address unique risks while maintaining the quality of user experience.

Blockchain technologies present unique security requirements that demand adaptation of traditional controls. The distributed nature of blockchain systems requires new approaches to security control implementation while maintaining the integrity of distributed ledger operations.

Success in adapting CIS Controls to emerging technologies depends on understanding both security principles and technological capabilities. Organizations must focus on security objectives while evolving their implementation approaches to address emerging technological challenges.

Scaling Security Strategies for Organizational Growth

Effective security scaling represents a critical challenge as organizations grow and evolve. Expanding security controls while maintaining effectiveness requires careful planning and systematic implementation approaches. Understanding how to scale security operations becomes increasingly important as organizations face growing complexity and expanding threat landscapes.

Security architecture plays a fundamental role in scalability. Properly designed security architectures must accommodate growth without requiring a complete redesign. This requires building flexibility into core security components, allowing expansion without disrupting existing operations. The architecture should support adding new capabilities and expanding coverage while maintaining consistent security control across the growing infrastructure.

Automation becomes increasingly critical as organizations scale. Manual security processes that work for small environments often become bottlenecks as organizations grow. Implementing automated security controls, monitoring, and response capabilities helps maintain security effectiveness while supporting organizational expansion. This automation must be designed to scale alongside the organization, handling increased load without degrading performance.

Identity and access management systems require particular attention during scaling. As organizations grow, managing user access becomes increasingly complex. Security controls must evolve to handle larger user populations, more complex access requirements, and growing numbers of systems and applications. This evolution demands robust identity management frameworks that scale effectively while maintaining security.

Security monitoring capabilities must scale with organizational growth. Security monitoring systems must handle increased data volumes as infrastructure expands while maintaining detection effectiveness. This requires implementing scalable logging and analysis capabilities that can grow with the organization. The monitoring infrastructure must support adding new data sources and expanding analysis capabilities without compromising performance.

Incident response processes need to scale effectively with organizational growth. As operations expand, security teams must handle more incidents across larger, more complex environments. This scaling requires developing robust incident response frameworks that can operate effectively at scale. Response procedures must remain effective while handling increased incident volumes and complexity.

Policy management becomes more challenging as organizations grow. Security policies must remain effective and enforceable across expanding operations. This requires developing scalable policy frameworks that maintain consistency while accommodating growth. The policy infrastructure must support adding new requirements and expanding coverage without becoming unwieldy.

Security training programs must scale to support growing organizations. As staff numbers increase and roles diversify, security awareness and training programs must expand effectively. This requires developing scalable training frameworks that maintain effectiveness while supporting larger user populations. The training infrastructure must accommodate growth while ensuring consistent security awareness across the organization.

Compliance management grows more complex with organizational expansion. As operations grow, organizations often face additional compliance requirements. Security controls must scale to address expanding compliance needs while maintaining efficiency. This requires implementing compliance frameworks that can grow with the organization while ensuring consistent control effectiveness.

Vendor management becomes increasingly important as organizations scale. Growing operations often involve more third-party relationships and dependencies. Security controls must scale to manage expanding vendor ecosystems effectively. This requires developing vendor management frameworks that maintain security effectiveness while supporting organizational growth.

Asset management complexity increases with organizational growth. As infrastructure expands, maintaining accurate asset inventory and control becomes more challenging. Security controls must scale to handle growing numbers of assets while maintaining effectiveness. This requires implementing asset management frameworks that can grow with the organization while ensuring consistent control.

Security budgeting must scale appropriately with organizational growth. As operations expand, security investments must grow proportionally to maintain effectiveness. This requires developing scalable budgeting frameworks that align security spending with organizational growth. The budgeting process must support expanding security capabilities while maintaining cost-effectiveness.

Risk management becomes more complex as organizations scale. Growing operations often introduce new risks and increase existing risk levels. Security controls must scale to address expanding risk landscapes while maintaining effectiveness. This requires implementing risk management frameworks that can grow with the organization while ensuring comprehensive risk coverage.

Documentation requirements expand with organizational growth. As operations become more complex, maintaining effective security documentation becomes more challenging. Security controls must scale to handle increased documentation needs while maintaining usability. This requires developing documentation frameworks to grow with the organization while ensuring information accessibility.

Success in scaling security operations often depends on balancing growth and control effectiveness. Organizations must develop scalable security frameworks that support expansion while ensuring consistent protection. This balance requires careful planning and systematic implementation of scalable security controls.

Chapter 12: Measuring Impact and Success

Key Performance Indicators (KPIs): Measuring Security Program Success

Measuring the effectiveness of CIS Controls implementation requires carefully designed Key Performance Indicators that provide meaningful insight into security program performance. Effective measurement frameworks combine technical metrics with business-aligned indicators to demonstrate security value and guide program improvements.

Security coverage metrics form a fundamental component of measurement frameworks. They assess the extent of control implementation across the organization's environment and track the percentage of assets, systems, and processes protected by specific controls. Coverage metrics must account for technical control deployment and process implementation to provide accurate visibility into the security program scope.

Control effectiveness metrics assess how well implemented controls perform their intended functions. These measurements evaluate control performance through various indicators, including detection rates, false positive rates, and response times. Effectiveness metrics help organizations understand whether controls deliver expected security improvements rather than simply tracking their presence.

Time-based measurements provide important insights into security program performance. These metrics track various time elements, including the mean time to detect incidents, the mean time to respond, and the mean time to resolve issues. Time-based metrics help organizations understand the operational efficiency of their security controls and identify areas needing improvement.

Compliance metrics track adherence to both internal security policies and external regulatory requirements. They assess how effectively controls maintain required compliance states and identify areas of potential non-compliance. To provide meaningful compliance visibility, compliance metrics must balance point-in-time measurements with trending analysis.

Risk reduction metrics evaluate how effectively security controls mitigate identified risks. These measurements track changes in risk levels over time and assess the impact of control implementations on overall risk posture. Risk metrics help organizations understand whether security investments reduce risk rather than simply implementing controls.

Operational impact metrics assess how security controls affect business operations. These measurements track various operational factors, including system performance impacts, user productivity effects, and process efficiency changes. Operational metrics help organizations understand the full impact of security controls beyond their security benefits.

Cost-effectiveness metrics evaluate the financial aspects of security control implementation. These measurements track both direct costs, such as tool investments, and indirect costs, such as operational impacts. Cost metrics help organizations understand the full financial impact of their security program and assess the return on security investment.

Incident metrics provide crucial insight into security program effectiveness. These measurements track various incident-related factors, including incident volumes, types, and impacts. Incident metrics help organizations understand how effectively their controls prevent, detect, and respond to security events.

User behavior metrics assess how effectively security controls influence user actions. These measurements track various behavior indicators, including policy compliance rates, security awareness levels, and reporting rates. Behavior metrics help organizations understand whether their controls effectively shape user security practices.

Asset management metrics evaluate how well organizations maintain control over their infrastructure. These measurements track various asset-related factors, including inventory accuracy, configuration compliance, and patch levels. Asset metrics help organizations understand their security foundation and identify potential vulnerabilities.

Access control metrics assess the effectiveness of authentication and authorization mechanisms. These measurements track access-related factors, including authentication success rates, privilege usage patterns, and access policy violations. Access metrics help organizations understand how effectively they control resource access.

Security awareness metrics evaluate the effectiveness of training and education programs. These measurements track awareness indicators, including training completion rates, assessment scores, and behavior changes. Awareness metrics help organizations understand whether their security education efforts improve security practices.

Technical debt metrics assess accumulating security issues that require attention. These measurements track various factors, including unpatched vulnerabilities, unresolved alerts, and pending security improvements. Technical debt metrics help organizations understand growing security risks that require attention.

Program maturity metrics evaluate overall security program development. These measurements track various maturity indicators, including process documentation, automation levels, and control sophistication. Maturity metrics help organizations understand their security program evolution and identify improvement opportunities.

Success in security measurement often depends on selecting appropriate metrics that provide meaningful insight while remaining practical to collect and analyze. Organizations must develop measurement frameworks that balance comprehensiveness with usability while providing actionable security insights.

Comprehensive Security KPI Definitions

Security Coverage KPIs:

- **Control Implementation Rate:** Percentage of planned controls fully implemented
- **Asset Protection Coverage:** Percentage of assets covered by security controls
- **Process Control Coverage:** Percentage of business processes with security controls
- **Network Coverage:** Percentage of network segments with security monitoring
- **System Protection Rate:** Percentage of systems with complete security stack

Control Effectiveness KPIs:

- **Control Detection Rate:** Percentage of known threats detected by controls
- **False Positive Rate:** Percentage of alerts that are false alarms
- **Control Bypass Rate:** Frequency of controls being circumvented
- **Alert Accuracy:** Percentage of valid security alerts
- **Control Failure Rate:** Frequency of control malfunctions or failures

Time-based KPIs:

- **Mean Time to Detect (MTTD):** Average time to identify security

CHAPTER 12: MEASURING IMPACT AND SUCCESS

incidents
- **Mean Time to Respond (MTTR):** Average time to initiate incident response
- **Mean Time to Resolve (MTTRes):** Average time to fully resolve incidents
- **Patch Implementation Time:** Average time to deploy critical patches
- **Alert Response Time:** Average time between alert and initial response

Compliance KPIs:

- **Policy Compliance Rate:** Percentage of systems meeting security policies
- **Regulatory Compliance Score:** Measured adherence to regulatory requirements
- **Audit Finding Resolution Rate:** Speed of addressing audit findings
- **Control Testing Coverage:** Percentage of controls regularly tested
- **Documentation Currency:** Percentage of documentation up to date

Risk Reduction KPIs:

- **Risk Score Trend:** Change in organizational risk scores over time
- **Vulnerability Closure Rate:** Speed of addressing identified vulnerabilities
- **High-Risk Finding Rate:** Number of high-risk issues identified
- **Risk Mitigation Effectiveness:** Measured reduction in risk after controls

- **Risk Assessment Coverage:** Percentage of assets with current risk assessments

Operational Impact KPIs:

- **System Performance Impact:** Measured effect on system performance
- **User Productivity Impact:** Effect on user workflow efficiency
- **Process Delay Rate:** Frequency of security-related process delays
- **System Availability Impact:** Effect on system uptime
- **Change Success Rate:** Percentage of security changes without issues

Cost Effectiveness KPIs:

- **Security Cost per Asset:** Security spending per protected asset
- **Investment Efficiency:** Security improvement per dollar spent
- **Operating Cost Trend:** Change in security operating costs
- **Tool Utilization Rate:** Usage levels of security investments
- **Cost Avoidance Metrics:** Measured savings from prevented incidents

Incident KPIs:

- **Incident Rate:** Number of security incidents per period
- **Incident Impact Levels:** Severity distribution of incidents
- **Repeat Incident Rate:** Frequency of similar incidents
- **Incident Recovery Cost:** Average cost per incident

CHAPTER 12: MEASURING IMPACT AND SUCCESS

- **Prevention Success Rate:** Percentage of prevented known attacks

User Behavior KPIs:

- **Security Violation Rate:** Frequency of policy violations
- **Reporting Rate:** Frequency of security issue reporting
- **Training Compliance:** Percentage of completed security training
- **Phishing Test Success:** Pass rate on phishing simulations
- **Password Policy Compliance:** Adherence to password requirements

Asset Management KPIs:

- **Inventory Accuracy:** Percentage accuracy of asset inventory
- **Configuration Compliance:** Percentage of correctly configured assets
- **Patch Compliance Rate:** Percentage of systems properly patched
- **Unauthorized Asset Rate:** Frequency of unauthorized device detection
- **Asset Management Coverage:** Percentage of assets under management

Access Control KPIs:

- **Authentication Success Rate:** Percentage of successful authentications
- **Privilege Violation Rate:** Frequency of access policy violations
- **Account Hygiene Level:** Measurement of account management

compliance
- **Access Review Coverage:** Percentage of access regularly reviewed
- **Unauthorized Access Attempts:** Frequency of access violations

Security Awareness KPIs:

- **Training Completion Rate:** Percentage of completed security training
- **Awareness Assessment Scores:** Results of security knowledge tests
- **Behavior Change Metrics:** Measured improvements in security practices
- **Reporting Accuracy:** Quality of security issue reports
- **Security Culture Score:** Measured security awareness level

Technical Debt KPIs:

- **Outstanding Vulnerability Count:** Number of unresolved vulnerabilities
- **Overdue Patch Count:** Number of missing critical patches
- **Unresolved Alert Count:** Number of pending security alerts
- **Legacy System Exposure:** Risk from outdated systems
- **Technical Debt Ratio:** Relationship between issues and resolutions

Program Maturity KPIs:

- **Documentation Completeness:** Percentage of documented processes

- **Automation Level:** Percentage of automated security processes
- **Control Sophistication:** Measured advancement of security controls
- **Process Maturity Score:** Assessment of process development
- **Program Coverage:** Completeness of security program implementation

Return on Security Investment (ROSI): Understanding Security Value

Return on Security Investment (ROSI) is a critical metric for demonstrating the business value of security programs. Understanding how to calculate and communicate ROSI helps security professionals justify investments and demonstrate program effectiveness. This complex calculation requires consideration of multiple factors, including risk reduction, cost avoidance, and operational improvements.

The fundamental ROSI calculation considers both monetary benefits and implementation costs. The basic formula examines the relationship between risk reduction and investment costs: ROSI = (Risk Reduction - Solution Cost) / Solution Cost. However, this simple calculation often fails to capture the full complexity of security investments. More comprehensive approaches must consider multiple value components and long-term impacts.

Risk reduction valuation forms a crucial component of ROSI calculations. Organizations must quantify the potential impact of security incidents they aim to prevent. This requires analyzing historical incident data, industry statistics, and organization-specific risk factors. The analysis should consider direct costs like incident response and indirect costs such as reputation damage and lost business opportunities.

Implementation costs extend beyond initial investments. Comprehensive cost analysis must consider ongoing operational expenses, maintenance requirements, and potential system impacts. Organizations should examine direct costs, such as tool licenses, and indirect costs, including effects on staff time and productivity. This complete cost picture provides more accurate ROSI calculations.

Operational benefits often provide significant ROSI contributions. Security improvements frequently deliver operational advantages beyond risk reduction. These benefits might include improved system performance, reduced maintenance requirements, or enhanced operational efficiency. Including these operational improvements in ROSI calculations provides a more accurate value assessment.

Compliance value requires specific consideration in ROSI calculations. Security investments often help organizations maintain regulatory compliance and avoid potential penalties. Compliance maintenance and violation prevention should be a factor in ROSI assessments. This compliance component often provides substantial justification for security investments.

Time factors significantly influence ROSI calculations. Security investments typically deliver benefits over extended periods while requiring upfront costs. ROSI calculations must consider this temporal aspect, examining both short-term impacts and long-term value delivery. This time-based analysis helps organizations understand investment value over different horizons.

Incident prevention value proves challenging to quantify. Organizations often struggle to demonstrate the value of prevented incidents. Effective ROSI calculations must incorporate reasonable estimates of prevented incident costs based on industry data and organizational experience. This prevention value often represents a substantial portion of security investment returns.

Productivity impacts require careful consideration. Security controls can either enhance or impede operational efficiency. ROSI calculations should examine these productivity effects, considering both positive and negative impacts. This productivity analysis helps organizations understand the full operational impact of security investments.

Asset protection value contributes to ROSI calculations. Security investments help protect organizational assets from damage or compromise. ROSI assessments should consider the value of protected assets and potential loss prevention. This protection value often provides substantial justification for security investments.

Reputation protection deserves specific attention. Security breaches can significantly damage organizational reputation. ROSI calculations should consider the value of reputation protection and potential breach impact prevention. This reputational component often justifies significant security investments.

Competitive advantage considerations affect ROSI assessments. Strong security programs can provide market advantages through enhanced customer trust and improved partner relationships. ROSI calculations should consider these competitive benefits when evaluating security investments.

Innovation support represents another ROSI component. Effective security programs enable organizations to innovate more freely by managing associated risks. ROSI calculations should consider how security investments support organizational innovation and growth.

Staff efficiency improvements contribute to ROSI. Security automation and process improvements often enhance staff productivity. ROSI calculations should examine these efficiency gains when evaluating security investments. This efficiency component often provides substantial return value.

Long-term cost avoidance requires specific attention. Security investments often prevent future costs related to incident response, system recovery, and compliance violations. ROSI calculations should consider these avoided future costs when assessing investment value.

Success in ROSI calculation often depends on balancing comprehensiveness and practicality. Organizations must develop ROSI frameworks that capture relevant value components while remaining practical to implement and understand. This balance helps organizations effectively demonstrate security investment value while maintaining calculation credibility.

CHAPTER 12: MEASURING IMPACT AND SUCCESS

Continuous Improvement Cycle: Maintaining and Enhancing Security Controls

Continuous improvement forms the backbone of effective security control management. Rather than viewing security implementation as a one-time project, organizations must establish systematic processes for ongoing evaluation and enhancement of their security controls. This continuous cycle ensures security measures remain effective against evolving threats while supporting organizational objectives.

The assessment phase initiates the continuous improvement cycle. Organizations must regularly evaluate their security controls' effectiveness through automated testing, manual validation, and performance monitoring. These assessments provide crucial data about control effectiveness, identifying strengths and areas needing improvement. The assessment process must examine technical control performance, operational impact, and business alignment.

The analysis follows an assessment of the improvement cycle. Organizations must carefully examine assessment data to identify patterns, trends, and potential issues. This analysis phase requires examining individual control performance and overall security program effectiveness. The analysis should consider various factors, including technical effectiveness, operational efficiency, and business impact. This comprehensive analysis helps organizations understand both immediate issues and longer-term improvement opportunities.

Planning represents a critical phase in the improvement cycle. Based on the analysis results, organizations must develop structured plans for implementing identified improvements. These plans should prioritize enhancements based on various factors, including risk levels, resource requirements, and potential impact. The planning phase must consider the proposed changes' technical feasibility and operational implications. This balanced approach helps ensure improvement initiatives deliver meaningful security enhancements while remaining practical to implement.

Implementation follows planning in the improvement cycle. Organizations must carefully execute planned improvements while maintaining existing security capabilities. This implementation phase requires careful coordination to ensure changes enhance rather than disrupt security operations. The implementation process should include appropriate testing and validation to confirm improvements achieve the intended objectives. This systematic approach helps organizations maintain security effectiveness during enhancement efforts.

Validation forms an essential part of the improvement cycle. Organizations must verify that implemented changes deliver expected improvements. This validation phase should examine various aspects, including technical effectiveness, operational impact, and business alignment. The validation process helps organizations confirm improvement value while identifying any necessary adjustments. This verification step ensures organizations achieve meaningful security enhancements from their improvement efforts.

Documentation plays a crucial role in continuous improvement. Organizations must maintain clear records of their improvement activities, including assessments, analyses, plans, and implementation results. This documentation provides an important historical context for future improvement efforts while supporting program governance. The documentation process should capture technical details and business impacts of security enhancements.

Metrics drive effective continuous improvement. Organizations must establish meaningful measurements for tracking both security effectiveness and improvement progress. These metrics should address technical performance, operational efficiency, and business value. The measurement framework helps organizations understand improvement impacts while identifying future enhancement opportunities.

Stakeholder engagement supports successful continuous improvement. Organizations must maintain effective communication with various stakeholders throughout the improvement cycle. This engagement ensures improvement efforts align with business needs while maintaining necessary support. The communication process should address both technical and business aspects of security enhancements.

Resource management requires careful attention to continuous improvement. Organizations must allocate appropriate resources for ongoing enhancement efforts while maintaining security operations. This resource planning should consider various needs, including staff time, technical tools, and financial requirements. The resource management process helps organizations maintain sustainable improvement programs.

Knowledge management supports effective improvement efforts. Organizations must capture and share insights gained through their improvement activities. This knowledge-sharing helps teams learn from experience while avoiding repeated issues. The knowledge management process should support both technical understanding and operational expertise development.

Cultural aspects significantly influence continuous improvement success. Organizations must develop cultures supporting ongoing security enhancement rather than viewing security as static. This cultural development requires promoting continuous learning and improvement mindsets throughout the organization. The cultural aspect helps maintain momentum for security enhancements.

Automation plays an increasing role in continuous improvement. Organizations should leverage automated tools for various improvement activities, including assessment, analysis, and implementation. This automation helps organizations maintain consistent improvement processes while optimizing resource utilization. The automation strategy should balance efficiency with appropriate human oversight.

Integration with other processes enhances improvement effectiveness. Organizations should connect their security improvement cycle with other operational processes, including change management, incident response, and risk management. This integration helps ensure coordinated enhancement efforts while maximizing the impact of improvement.

Success in continuous improvement often depends on maintaining consistent focus while adapting to changing requirements. Organizations must develop sustainable improvement processes that deliver ongoing security enhancements while remaining practical. This balance helps organizations achieve meaningful security improvements over time.

Closing

Key Takeaways: Critical Elements for Successful CIS Controls Implementation

The successful implementation of CIS Controls requires understanding and applying several fundamental principles that remain consistent across different organizational contexts. These critical elements for success emerge from extensive implementation experience and represent essential considerations for any organization seeking to enhance its security posture through CIS Controls.

Understanding control interdependencies represents a fundamental success factor. Controls do not exist in isolation but form an interconnected framework where effectiveness often depends on properly implementing supporting controls. For instance, asset management controls provide the foundation for numerous other security measures. Without accurate asset inventory, organizations cannot effectively implement controls for configuration management, vulnerability assessment, or access control. Recognizing and properly managing these dependencies helps organizations develop more effective implementation strategies.

Proper prioritization plays a crucial role in implementation success. When determining the implementation order, organizations must balance various factors, including risk levels, resource requirements, and operational impact. The Implementation Group (IG) framework provided by CIS helps organizations understand appropriate starting points and progression paths. However, organizations must also consider their specific circumstances when prioritizing control implementation. This balanced approach helps ensure security improvements align with risk management needs and operational capabilities.

Resource allocation significantly influences implementation outcomes. Organizations must realistically assess and allocate resources across various control implementation needs. This includes financial resources, staff time, technical capabilities, and operational capacity. Understanding the full resource requirements for implementation and ongoing maintenance helps organizations develop sustainable security programs. This comprehensive resource planning prevents common issues like incomplete implementations or degrading controls due to insufficient support.

Technical architecture considerations fundamentally affect implementation success. Organizations must develop security architectures that support effective control implementation while maintaining operational efficiency. This requires understanding both current technical requirements and future scalability needs. Proper architecture planning helps organizations implement effective controls as their environment evolves. This forward-looking approach prevents the need for frequent major restructuring of security controls.

Process integration represents another critical success factor. Security controls must integrate effectively with various operational processes, including change management, incident response, and business workflows. This integration ensures security measures enhance rather than hinder organizational operations. Understanding and properly managing these process interactions helps organizations maintain security effectiveness and operational efficiency.

Documentation practices significantly impact long-term success. Organizations must maintain comprehensive documentation covering various aspects, including implementation details, operational procedures, and maintenance requirements. This documentation supports both operational consistency and knowledge transfer. Proper documentation helps organizations maintain effective controls even as staff changes occur and systems evolve.

Measurement capabilities prove essential for demonstrating success. Organizations must develop effective methods for measuring both implementation progress and control effectiveness. These measurements should address technical performance, operational impact, and business value. Proper metrics help organizations understand their security posture while identifying improvement opportunities.

Stakeholder management fundamentally affects implementation success. Organizations must effectively engage various stakeholders, including executive leadership, technical staff, and end users. This engagement ensures necessary support while helping align security improvements with business needs. Understanding and properly managing stakeholder expectations helps organizations maintain implementation momentum.

Continuous improvement mechanisms ensure long-term effectiveness. Organizations must establish processes for regularly evaluating and enhancing their security controls. This ongoing improvement helps organizations address evolving threats while maintaining security effectiveness. Understanding the need for continuous enhancement prevents security controls from becoming outdated or ineffective.

Training and awareness programs support implementation success. Organizations must develop effective methods for building and maintaining security knowledge across various roles. This includes technical training for security staff and awareness programs for general users. Proper training helps organizations maintain security effectiveness while promoting secure behaviors.

Compliance management requires careful attention. Organizations must understand how CIS Controls implementation relates to various compliance requirements. This understanding helps organizations leverage control implementations to satisfy multiple compliance needs. Proper compliance management prevents duplicate efforts while ensuring regulatory requirements receive appropriate attention.

Incident response capabilities significantly influence success. Organizations must develop effective methods for detecting and responding to security incidents, including both technical capabilities and operational procedures. Proper incident response helps organizations maintain security effectiveness while learning from security events.

Change management practices affect implementation sustainability. Organizations must establish effective processes for managing security changes while maintaining operational stability. This includes both technical changes and procedural modifications. Proper change management helps organizations implement improvements while preventing disruptions.

Success in CIS Controls implementation ultimately depends on balancing various requirements while adapting to specific organizational needs. Organizations must develop implementation approaches that deliver effective security improvements while remaining practical. This balanced approach helps organizations achieve meaningful security enhancements while supporting business objectives.

The Journey Ahead: Maintaining Security Excellence

Implementing CIS Controls represents not a destination but the beginning of an ongoing security journey. As technology evolves and threats emerge, organizations must maintain their commitment to security excellence while adapting to new challenges. This forward-looking perspective helps organizations build and maintain robust security postures that support their ongoing success.

Security evolution requires continuous attention and adaptation. The threat landscape constantly changes as attackers develop new techniques and exploit emerging vulnerabilities. Organizations must maintain awareness of these evolving threats while continuously enhancing their security capabilities. This ongoing evolution helps organizations avoid potential threats rather than respond to known issues.

Technology advancement creates both opportunities and challenges for security programs. New technologies offer enhanced capabilities for protecting organizational assets but also introduce potential vulnerabilities. Organizations must carefully evaluate these technological changes while maintaining effective security controls. This balanced approach helps organizations leverage new capabilities while managing associated risks.

Organizational growth introduces new security considerations. As organizations expand their operations, they often face new security challenges, including increased complexity, additional compliance requirements, and emerging threats. Security programs must evolve to address these changing needs while maintaining consistent protection. This scalable approach helps organizations maintain security effectiveness during growth.

Business transformation affects security requirements. Organizations frequently undergo various transformations, including digital initiatives, operational changes, and market expansions. Security programs must adapt to support these transformations while maintaining robust protection. This adaptive approach helps organizations enable business innovation while managing security risks.

Regulatory landscapes continue to evolve, and organizations often face new compliance requirements as regulations change and expand. Security programs must adapt to address these evolving requirements while maintaining operational effectiveness. This compliance-aware approach helps organizations satisfy regulatory needs while optimizing security investments.

Skill development requires ongoing attention. Security technologies and practices continue to advance, requiring continuous learning and skill enhancement. Organizations must maintain effective training programs while supporting professional development. This learning-focused approach helps security teams maintain the necessary capabilities while adapting to new challenges.

Resource optimization remains an ongoing challenge. Organizations must continuously balance security needs with available resources, including budget, staff, and technical capabilities. Security programs must maintain effectiveness while optimizing resource utilization. This efficient approach helps organizations achieve maximum security value from their investments.

Partnership development supports security enhancement. Organizations often benefit from various security partnerships, including vendor relationships, information-sharing communities, and professional networks. These partnerships provide valuable resources for maintaining and enhancing security capabilities. This collaborative approach helps organizations leverage collective knowledge while addressing common challenges.

Cultural enhancement supports security effectiveness. Organizations must maintain security-aware cultures that support ongoing protection efforts. This includes promoting security consciousness, encouraging responsible behavior, and maintaining stakeholder engagement. This cultural approach helps organizations maintain security effectiveness through shared responsibility.

Adoption of innovation requires careful consideration. Organizations must evaluate and implement security innovations while maintaining operational stability. This includes assessing new security technologies, methodologies, and practices. This innovative approach helps organizations enhance their security capabilities while managing associated risks.

Knowledge management supports ongoing improvement. Organizations must maintain effective methods for capturing and sharing security knowledge, including implementation experiences, incident lessons, and best practices. This knowledge-sharing approach helps organizations build upon their security experiences while avoiding repeated issues.

Measurement evolution ensures continued relevance. Organizations must maintain effective methods for measuring security performance while adapting metrics to address changing needs. This includes evaluating both technical effectiveness and business value. This measurement approach helps organizations demonstrate security value while identifying improvement opportunities.

Leadership engagement remains crucial for success. Organizations must maintain executive support for security initiatives while demonstrating ongoing value. This includes effective communication of security achievements and requirements. This engagement approach helps organizations maintain necessary resources while aligning security with business objectives.

The security journey continues with each new day, bringing challenges and enhancement opportunities. Organizations that maintain their commitment to security excellence while adapting to change will be better prepared for future challenges. This ongoing journey represents not a burden but an opportunity to strengthen organizational resilience and support continued success.

As you continue your security journey, remember that each step forward enhances your organization's protection while building capabilities for future challenges. Maintain your commitment to

CLOSING

security excellence, stay engaged with security communities, and continue learning from successes and challenges. Your dedication to robust security helps protect not just your organization but contributes to the overall security of our interconnected world.

Appendix A: Glossary of Cybersecurity Terms

Access Control: A security technique that regulates who or what can view, use, or access resources in a computing environment. This includes the rules governing access and the mechanisms enforcing these rules.

Advanced Persistent Threat (APT): A sophisticated cyber attack where an unauthorized user gains network access and stays undetected for an extended period. APTs typically focus on stealing data rather than causing immediate damage.

Asset Management: The systematic process of deploying, maintaining, upgrading, and disposing of organizational assets. In cybersecurity, this includes both physical and digital assets requiring protection.

Authentication: The process of verifying the identity of a user, device, or system. This can involve various factors, including passwords, biometrics, or security tokens.

Authorization: Determining an authenticated entity's permissions within a system. This includes what resources they can access and what actions they can perform.

APPENDIX A: GLOSSARY OF CYBERSECURITY TERMS

Backdoor: A method of bypassing normal authentication in a system, providing unauthorized remote access. These can be intentionally created for maintenance or maliciously installed by attackers.

Baseline Configuration: A documented, standard set of specifications for systems or applications. This serves as a reference point for secure configurations and future changes.

Bitcoin: A decentralized digital currency that uses cryptography for security. Often referenced in cybersecurity regarding ransomware payments or cryptocurrency-based attacks.

Blockchain: A distributed ledger technology that maintains a growing list of records (blocks) linked using cryptography. Each block contains transaction data and a timestamp.

Botnet: A compromised computer network controlled by an attacker, typically used for malicious purposes such as distributed denial-of-service attacks.

Certificate Authority (CA): An entity that issues digital certificates that verify the ownership of public keys used in secure communications.

Cloud Computing: The delivery of computing services over the internet, including servers, storage, databases, networking, and software.

Configuration Management: The process of maintaining systems, including hardware and software, in a known, consistent state. This helps ensure security controls remain effective.

Cryptography: The practice of securing information by transforming it into an unreadable format, which can only be decoded by authorized parties.

Data Loss Prevention (DLP): Technologies and processes that ensure unauthorized users don't lose, misuse, or access sensitive data.

Distributed Denial-of-Service (DDoS): An attack where multiple compromised systems target a single system, causing service disruption through overwhelming traffic.

Encryption: The process of converting information into a coded form to prevent unauthorized access. This can be applied to data in transit or at rest.

Endpoint Protection: Security approach focusing on network endpoints like laptops, mobile devices, and workstations. This includes antivirus, firewall, and other security measures.

Exploit: A piece of software, chunk of data, or sequence of commands that takes advantage of a vulnerability to cause unintended behavior.

Firewall: A network security device that monitors and controls incoming and outgoing network traffic based on predetermined security rules.

Fuzzing: A software testing technique that provides invalid, unexpected, or random data as inputs to a computer program to find security vulnerabilities.

Governance: The system by which an organization directs and controls

APPENDIX A: GLOSSARY OF CYBERSECURITY TERMS

IT security, including frameworks, policies, and procedures.

Hardening: The process of securing a system by reducing its vulnerability and attack surface through configuration changes and security controls.

Incident Response: The organized approach to addressing and managing the aftermath of a security breach or attack. This includes preparation, detection, analysis, and recovery.

Intrusion Detection System (IDS): A device or application that monitors network traffic for malicious activity or policy violations and generates alerts when detected.

Intrusion Prevention System (IPS): Similar to IDS but can also take automated actions to prevent detected threats.

Malware: Software designed to damage, disrupt, or gain unauthorized access to computer systems. This includes viruses, worms, trojans, and ransomware.

Multi-Factor Authentication (MFA): An authentication method requiring two or more independent ways of proving identity.

Patch Management: The systematic process of acquiring, testing, and installing code updates on existing applications and software tools.

Penetration Testing: An authorized simulated attack on a computer system to evaluate its security. Also known as ethical hacking.

Phishing: A cyber attack that uses disguised email as a weapon to trick recipients into revealing sensitive information.

Ransomware: Malicious software that encrypts victims' files, with attackers demanding payment for decryption.

Risk Assessment: The process of identifying, analyzing, and evaluating risk to inform decisions about actions.

Security Information and Event Management (SIEM): A system providing real-time analysis of security alerts generated by various hardware and software.

Social Engineering: The psychological manipulation of people into performing actions or divulging confidential information.

Threat Intelligence: Evidence-based knowledge about existing or emerging threats to assets.

Vulnerability: A weakness in a system that could be exploited to compromise security.

Zero-Day: A previously unknown security vulnerability in software, typically discovered when exploited by attackers before developers can create patches.

Zero Trust: A security concept centered on the belief that organizations shouldn't automatically trust anything inside or outside their perimeters.

Appendix B: List of Acronyms with Explanations

ABAC (Attribute-Based Access Control): A security model that evaluates attributes (user, resource, environment) to determine access permissions.

ACS (Access Control System): A system that manages and controls access to physical or digital resources based on defined policies.

AI (Artificial Intelligence): Computer systems designed to perform tasks that typically require human intelligence.

APT (Advanced Persistent Threat): A sophisticated cyber attack where an unauthorized actor maintains long-term access to a network.

BYOD (Bring Your Own Device): A policy allowing employees to use personal devices for work purposes.

CASB (Cloud Access Security Broker): Security enforcement points between cloud service users and providers.

CERT (Computer Emergency Response Team): A group of experts who handle computer security incidents.

CIA (Confidentiality, Integrity, Availability): The three fundamental information security principles.

CIS (Center for Internet Security): Organization that develops security best practices and controls.

CMDB (Configuration Management Database): Database containing information about hardware and software assets.

CSIRT (Computer Security Incident Response Team): Group responsible for responding to security incidents.

CSOC (Cybersecurity Operations Center): Facility where security analysts monitor and defend against cyber threats.

CVE (Common Vulnerabilities and Exposures): Standard identifiers for publicly known security vulnerabilities.

CVSS (Common Vulnerability Scoring System): Standard for rating the severity of security vulnerabilities.

DAST (Dynamic Application Security Testing): A testing method that analyzes running applications for vulnerabilities.

DDoS (Distributed Denial of Service): An attack that disrupts service by overwhelming systems with traffic from multiple sources.

DLP (Data Loss Prevention): Systems that detect and prevent unauthorized data exfiltration.

**DMARC (Domain-based Message Authentication, Reporting, and

APPENDIX B: LIST OF ACRONYMS WITH EXPLANATIONS

Conformance): Email authentication protocol.

DNS (Domain Name System): A system that translates domain names to IP addresses.

DKIM (DomainKeys Identified Mail): Email authentication method using digital signatures.

EDR (Endpoint Detection and Response): Advanced endpoint security tools that detect and investigate threats.

EPP (Endpoint Protection Platform): Security software that protects end-user devices.

FAIR (Factor Analysis of Information Risk): Framework for understanding and analyzing information risk.

FIM (File Integrity Monitoring): System that monitors file changes to detect unauthorized modifications.

FIPS (Federal Information Processing Standards): U.S. government standards for computer security.

FISMA (Federal Information Security Management Act): Law defining federal information security standards.

GDPR (General Data Protection Regulation): European Union data protection and privacy regulation.

GRC (Governance, Risk, and Compliance): Unified approach to organizational governance, risk management, and compliance.

HIPAA (Health Insurance Portability and Accountability Act): U.S. healthcare data privacy and security law.

HTTPS (Hypertext Transfer Protocol Secure): Secure version of HTTP using encryption.

IAM (Identity and Access Management): Framework for managing digital identities and access.

ICS (Industrial Control Systems): Systems used to monitor and control industrial processes.

IdM (Identity Management): Systems and processes for managing digital identities.

IDS (Intrusion Detection System): A system that monitors network traffic for suspicious activity.

IG (Implementation Group): CIS Controls classification based on organizational security requirements.

IoT (Internet of Things): Network of internet-connected physical devices.

IP (Internet Protocol): Core protocol of Internet communications.

IPS (Intrusion Prevention System): A system that monitors and blocks suspicious network activity.

ISAC (Information Sharing and Analysis Center): Organizations facilitating cyber threat information sharing.

APPENDIX B: LIST OF ACRONYMS WITH EXPLANATIONS

ISMS (Information Security Management System): Systematic approach to managing sensitive information.

ISO (International Organization for Standardization): Organization that develops international standards.

KPI (Key Performance Indicator): Measurable values that demonstrate effectiveness in achieving objectives.

KRI (Key Risk Indicator): Metrics that indicate potential risk levels.

LDAP (Lightweight Directory Access Protocol): Protocol for accessing and maintaining directory services.

LMS (Learning Management System): Software for administering and tracking training programs.

MDM (Mobile Device Management): Software for managing and securing mobile devices.

MFA (Multi-Factor Authentication): Authentication that requires multiple verification methods.

ML (Machine Learning): Systems that improve automatically through experience.

MSSP (Managed Security Service Provider): Companies providing outsourced security monitoring and management.

MTTR (Mean Time to Respond): Average time between alert detection and initial response.

MTTRes (Mean Time to Resolve): Average time to fully resolve security incidents.

NAC (Network Access Control): System controlling network access based on device policy compliance.

NDR (Network Detection and Response): Advanced network security monitoring and response platform.

NIST (National Institute of Standards and Technology): U.S. agency that develops technology standards.

OWASP (Open Web Application Security Project): Organization focused on web application security.

PAM (Privileged Access Management): Systems managing privileged account access.

PCI DSS (Payment Card Industry Data Security Standard): Security standards for payment card processing.

PHI (Protected Health Information): Individually identifiable health information.

PII (Personally Identifiable Information): Information that can identify specific individuals.

RBAC (Role-Based Access Control): Access control based on user roles.

ROI (Return on Investment): Measure of investment profitability.

APPENDIX B: LIST OF ACRONYMS WITH EXPLANATIONS

ROSI (Return on Security Investment): Measure of security investment effectiveness.

SAML (Security Assertion Markup Language): Standard for exchanging authentication data.

SAST (Static Application Security Testing): Testing of application source code for security issues.

SCA (Software Composition Analysis): Process of identifying third-party components of an application.

SCADA (Supervisory Control and Data Acquisition): Industrial control system architecture.

SCD (Secure Configuration Documentation): Documentation of security configuration standards.

SDLC (Software Development Life Cycle): Process for planning and creating software systems.

SIEM (Security Information and Event Management): System collecting and analyzing security alerts.

SLA (Service Level Agreement): Contract defining service delivery expectations.

SOAR (Security Orchestration, Automation, and Response): Tools automating security operations.

SOC (Security Operations Center): Facility monitoring and managing security operations.

SPF (Sender Policy Framework): Email authentication protocol.

SSO (Single Sign-On): Authentication allowing access to multiple systems with one login.

TLS (Transport Layer Security): Cryptographic protocol securing network communications.

TPM (Trusted Platform Module): Hardware-based security chip.

UAT (User Acceptance Testing): Testing phase validating system usability.

URL (Uniform Resource Locator): Web address specifying resource location.

VPN (Virtual Private Network): Encrypted network connection over public infrastructure.

VAPT (Vulnerability Assessment and Penetration Testing): Security testing combining vulnerability scanning and exploitation.

WAF (Web Application Firewall): Firewall protecting web applications.

WORM (Write Once Read Many): Data storage that cannot be modified once written.

XDR (Extended Detection and Response): Unified security incident detection and response.

APPENDIX B: LIST OF ACRONYMS WITH EXPLANATIONS

ZTNA (Zero Trust Network Access): Security model trusting nothing by default.

These acronyms represent fundamental concepts in cybersecurity and information technology. Understanding them is crucial for effectively implementing and managing security controls. The explanations provided offer context for their use in security documentation and discussions.

Appendix C: CIS Controls Implementation Resources

A comprehensive resource directory helps organizations identify and leverage appropriate tools and communities for their security implementation journey. This directory focuses on validated resources that provide practical value for CIS Controls implementation.

Network Security and Monitoring Tools

The **Nmap Security Scanner** provides essential capabilities for asset discovery and network mapping. This open-source tool supports various Control 1 requirements through comprehensive network scanning capabilities. Organizations can leverage basic scanning features and advanced NSE scripts for detailed asset discovery and validation.

Wireshark network protocol analyzer offers deep visibility into network traffic patterns. This tool proves particularly valuable for implementing Control 13's network monitoring requirements. Organizations can use Wireshark for routine traffic analysis and detailed protocol investigation during security incidents.

Security Configuration and Assessment

APPENDIX C: CIS CONTROLS IMPLEMENTATION RESOURCES

The **CIS-CAT Pro Assessor** helps organizations validate their security configurations against CIS benchmarks. This tool provides automated assessment capabilities for various platforms and applications. Organizations can leverage CIS-CAT Pro to verify compliance with security configuration requirements across multiple controls.

OpenVAS (Open Vulnerability Assessment System) provides comprehensive vulnerability scanning capabilities. This open-source tool supports Control 7 requirements through automated vulnerability detection and assessment. Organizations can use OpenVAS to maintain continuous visibility into their security posture.

Security Information and Event Management

The **ELK Stack (Elasticsearch, Logstash, Kibana)** provides robust log management and analysis capabilities. This open-source platform supports Control 8 requirements through centralized log collection and analysis. Organizations can leverage ELK Stack for both security monitoring and compliance documentation.

Wazuh offers comprehensive security monitoring and threat detection capabilities. This platform combines security functions, including log analysis, file integrity monitoring, and vulnerability detection. Organizations can use Wazuh to address requirements across multiple CIS Controls.

Professional Communities and Forums

The **CIS WorkBench** community provides direct access to CIS Controls expertise. This platform allows organizations to engage with other implementers and share implementation experiences. Members can access various resources, including implementation guides and discussion forums.

The **SANS Internet Storm Center** offers valuable threat intelligence and security guidance. This community provides daily updates on emerging threats and practical security advice. Organizations can leverage this resource to maintain awareness of current security challenges.

Training and Education Resources

The **CIS Controls Self Assessment Tool** helps organizations evaluate their implementation progress. This resource provides structured assessment capabilities across all CIS Controls. Organizations can use this tool to identify gaps and prioritize improvement efforts.

The **SANS Institute** offers comprehensive security training aligned with CIS Controls. Their courses cover various aspects of security implementation and management. Organizations can leverage these resources for staff development and skills enhancement.

Vulnerability Management Resources

The **National Vulnerability Database (NVD)** provides comprehensive vulnerability information. This resource supports Control 7 implementation through detailed vulnerability data and analysis. Organizations can integrate NVD data into their vulnerability management processes.

The **Exploit Database** maintains current information about security exploits and vulnerabilities. This resource helps organizations understand potential threats to their systems. Security teams can use this information for vulnerability prioritization and risk assessment.

Configuration Management Tools

Ansible provides automated configuration management capabilities. This tool supports various controls related to system configuration and maintenance. Organizations can leverage Ansible to maintain consistent security configurations across their infrastructure.

Puppet offers enterprise-grade configuration management features. This platform helps organizations maintain security configurations at scale. Teams can use Puppet to automate security control implementation and maintenance.

Documentation and Collaboration

The **CIS Controls Documentation Repository** provides implementation guidance and templates. This resource includes detailed documentation for each control and various implementation scenarios. Organizations can leverage these materials to develop their security documentation.

The **CIS Controls Community Wiki** maintains current implementation knowledge and best practices. This collaborative platform allows organizations to share implementation experiences and solutions. Teams can contribute to and benefit from shared community knowledge.

Incident Response Resources

The **SANS Incident Response Handbook** provides comprehensive guidance for security incident management. This resource supports

Control 17 implementation through detailed response procedures. Organizations can adapt these materials for their incident response programs.

The **FIRST (Forum of Incident Response and Security Teams)** community offers valuable incident response resources. This international organization provides various tools and best practices for incident management, which teams can leverage to enhance their incident response capabilities.

Continuous Improvement Resources

The **CIS Controls Assessment Module** helps organizations measure their security program maturity. This tool provides structured assessment capabilities for evaluating control effectiveness, and organizations can use this resource for ongoing program improvement.

The **CIS Controls Navigator** supports detailed control mapping and implementation planning. This tool helps organizations understand control relationships and dependencies. Teams can leverage this resource for implementation planning and progress tracking.

Appendix D: Recommended Reading and Resources

Foundation Cybersecurity Works

"Security Engineering: A Guide to Building Dependable Distributed Systems, Third Edition" by Ross Anderson (Wiley, 2020) serves as a cornerstone text in the field. Anderson's comprehensive work covers theoretical foundations and practical applications, making it essential reading for security professionals at all levels.

"The Practice of Network Security Monitoring: Understanding Incident Detection and Response" by Richard Bejtlich (No Starch Press, 2013) delivers practical insights into security monitoring implementation. Bejtlich's experience in real-world security operations provides a valuable perspective for practitioners.

"Applied Cryptography: Protocols, Algorithms, and Source Code in C" by Bruce Schneier (Wiley, 2015) remains a definitive resource for understanding cryptographic principles. Schneier's clear explanations make complex cryptographic concepts accessible to technical practitioners.

Technical Implementation Guides

"NIST Special Publication 800-53 Rev. 5: Security Controls Implementation" by Ron Ross, Victoria Pillitteri, and others (NIST, 2020) provides authoritative guidance on security control implementation. This comprehensive publication offers detailed implementation guidance aligned with federal standards.

"Blue Team Handbook: Incident Response Edition" by Don Murdoch (CreateSpace Independent Publishing Platform, 2014) offers practical guidance for security operations. Murdoch's hands-on approach provides immediately applicable techniques for incident response.

"The Web Application Hacker's Handbook: Finding and Exploiting Security Flaws" by Dafydd Stuttard and Marcus Pinto (Wiley, 2011) remains relevant for understanding web application security. Their detailed examination of web vulnerabilities helps security professionals implement effective controls.

Risk Management Resources

"Measuring and Managing Information Risk: A FAIR Approach" by Jack Freund and Jack Jones (Butterworth-Heinemann, 2014) introduces quantitative risk analysis methods. Their structured approach to risk assessment provides practical tools for security decision-making.

"Risk Management Framework: A Lab-Based Approach to Securing Information Systems" by James Broad (Syngress, 2013) offers hands-on guidance for implementing risk management. Broad's practical approach helps organizations develop effective risk management programs.

Security Architecture References

APPENDIX D: RECOMMENDED READING AND RESOURCES

"Enterprise Security Architecture: A Business-Driven Approach" by John Sherwood, Andrew Clark, and David Lynas (CRC Press, 2005) provides comprehensive architectural guidance. Their SABSA framework offers a structured approach to security architecture development.

"Zero Trust Networks: Building Secure Systems in Untrusted Networks" by Evan Gilman and Doug Barth (O'Reilly Media, 2017) explores modern security architectures. Their practical guidance helps organizations effectively implement zero-trust principles.

Incident Response Resources

"Incident Response & Computer Forensics" by Jason T. Luttgens, Matthew Pepe, and Kevin Mandia (McGraw-Hill Education, 2014) provides comprehensive incident response guidance. Their combined expertise offers practical insights for incident handling.

"Applied Incident Response" by Steve Anson (Wiley, 2020) presents current approaches to incident response. Anson's real-world experience informs practical guidance for response program development.

Security Operations Guides

"Security Operations Center Guidebook: A Practical Guide for a Successful SOC" by Gregory Jarpey and Scott McCoy (Packt Publishing, 2017) offers practical SOC implementation guidance. Their experience in building SOCs provides valuable insights for organizations.

"Network Security Monitoring: Basics for Beginners" by Chris Sanders (CreateSpace Independent Publishing Platform, 2011) introduces fundamental monitoring concepts. Sanders' clear explanations help organizations implement effective monitoring programs.

Compliance and Audit Resources

"Information Security Policies and Procedures: A Practitioner's Reference" by Thomas R. Peltier (Auerbach Publications, 2016) provides comprehensive policy guidance. Peltier's practical approach helps organizations develop effective security documentation.

"IT Auditing: Using Controls to Protect Information Assets" by Chris Davis, Mike Schiller, and Kevin Wheeler (McGraw-Hill Education, 2011) offers detailed audit guidance. Their combined experience provides valuable insights for control assessment.

Online Learning Platforms

SANS Institute courses, developed by industry experts like Ed Skoudis, Eric Conrad, and Johannes Ullrich, provide technical depth and practical application. Their hands-on approach ensures learning translates to practical skills.

Cybrary courses offer flexible learning options and feature instructors like Kelly Handerhan and Ken Underhill. Their platform provides both breadth and depth in security education.

These resources, created by recognized experts in their respective fields, provide comprehensive coverage of topics essential for effective CIS Controls implementation. Security professionals should select resources aligned with their needs while considering the authors' expertise and perspective.

About the Author

Edgardo Fernandez Climent, an accomplished IT leader with over two decades of experience, has significantly contributed to infrastructure, networks, and cybersecurity. His exceptional leadership skills and strategic vision have positioned him as a prominent figure in the industry. After graduating with honors in Computer Information Systems, Edgardo pursued an MBA and a Master's in Management Information Systems, further enhancing his expertise. He also holds several industry certifications, such as PMP, ITIL4, and Security+, demonstrating his commitment to professional development and staying at the forefront of industry standards.

Edgardo has consistently demonstrated his ability to lead organizations through complex technological transformations throughout his career. His deep understanding of emerging technologies and industry trends has enabled him to develop and implement innovative strategies that drive business growth and ensure technological resilience. Edgardo's leadership in navigating the ever-changing landscape of cybersecurity has been instrumental in safeguarding organizations against the evolving threats of the digital world.

As a visionary leader, Edgardo is known for his ability to inspire and motivate teams to achieve excellence. He fosters a culture of continuous learning and encourages his team members to embrace new technologies and develop their skills. Edgardo's commitment to mentoring and developing the next generation of IT leaders has profoundly impacted the industry as he shares his knowledge and experiences to empower others to succeed.

Edgardo's leadership style is characterized by his ability to build strong relationships, promote collaboration, and drive results. He has a proven track record of successfully leading cross-functional teams and aligning IT initiatives with business objectives. His strategic thinking and technical expertise have enabled him to develop and execute transformative initiatives that have delivered significant value to the organizations he has served.

Today, as a highly sought-after consultant in the IT industry, Edgardo continues to shape the technological landscape. His leadership and expertise are highly valued by organizations seeking to drive innovation, optimize their IT infrastructure, and strengthen their cybersecurity posture. Edgardo's journey is a testament to the power of visionary leadership, continuous learning, and a relentless pursuit of excellence in the ever-evolving field of information technology.

You can connect with me on:
- https://fernandezcliment.com
- https://twitter.com/efernandezclime
- https://www.facebook.com/edgardo.fernandez.climent
- https://amazon.com/author/efernandezcliment

Subscribe to my newsletter:

✉ https://fernandezcliment.com/join-our-mail-list

Also by Edgardo Fernandez Climent

Securing Operational Technology: Protecting Industrial Systems in the Digital Age

Dive into the critical Operational Technology (OT) security world with this comprehensive guide. As our industrial systems become increasingly connected, the need for robust cybersecurity measures has never been more urgent. This book offers a deep dive into the unique challenges and solutions for protecting the systems that run our power plants, manufacturing facilities, and critical infrastructure.

Written by an experienced IT & OT security specialist, this book bridges the gap between traditional IT security and the specialized needs of industrial control systems. Whether you're an OT engineer looking to enhance your security knowledge or a cybersecurity professional aiming to understand the intricacies of industrial environments, this book provides the insights and practical knowledge you need.

Key topics covered include:
   - The evolving landscape of OT and IT convergence
   - Comprehensive overview of OT-specific cybersecurity threats
   - Strategies for securing legacy systems without disrupting operations
   - Implementing effective network segmentation and access control
   - Best practices for incident response in OT environments
   - Navigating regulatory compliance in industrial sectors
   - Future trends in OT security, including AI and machine learning applications

Packed with real-world case studies, practical checklists, and in-depth explanations, this book is a thorough introduction for beginners and a valuable reference for experienced professionals. By the end, you'll have a solid foundation in OT security principles and the tools to implement a robust security program in your industrial environment.

Don't let your critical systems become the next cybersecurity headline. Equip yourself with the knowledge to protect our industrial backbone in the digital age. Get your copy of **"Securing Operational Technology"** today and take the first step towards a more secure industrial future.

NIST SP 800-37 Rev 2 Unlocked: Practical Risk Management Framework Implementation Strategies

In today's rapidly evolving digital landscape, effective risk management is more crucial than ever. "NIST SP 800-37 Rev 2 Unlocked: Practical Risk Management Framework Implementation Strategies" is your definitive guide to mastering the Risk Management Framework (RMF) as outlined by the National Institute of Standards and Technology (NIST). Whether you're a cybersecurity professional, an IT manager, or a federal contractor, this comprehensive handbook will equip you with the knowledge and tools necessary to protect your information systems against a myriad of threats.

What You'll Discover Inside:

- **In-Depth RMF Process:** Gain a thorough understanding of each step in the RMF process, from categorizing information systems to selecting, implementing, assessing, authorizing, and continuously monitoring security controls. Learn how to integrate these steps into your organization's security strategy effectively.

- **Real-World Case Studies:** Explore detailed examples of RMF implementation in federal and private sector organizations. Understand the unique challenges and successful strategies employed to overcome them, providing you with practical insights that can be directly applied to your projects.

- **Hands-On Exercises:** Use practical exercises to reinforce key concepts and methodologies. Develop and refine your skills in creating RMF project plans, categorizing information systems, developing risk management strategies, and conducting security control assessments.

- **Best Practices and Common Pitfalls:** Benefit from expert advice on best practices for RMF implementation, including tips for avoiding common pitfalls. Learn how to tailor security controls to your specific needs, leverage automation and technology, and foster a culture of continuous improvement within your organization.

- **Future Trends in Risk Management:** Stay ahead of the curve by exploring emerging trends and technologies in risk management. Understand the implications of AI and machine learning, Zero Trust Architecture, cloud security, blockchain, and quantum computing on your security posture. Prepare for future cybersecurity challenges with proactive strategies and advanced tools.

Who This Book Is For:

- **Cybersecurity Professionals:** Enhance your expertise in implementing and managing robust security frameworks.

- **IT Managers and Executives:** Equip yourself with the knowledge to make informed decisions about risk management and compliance.

- **Federal Contractors:** Ensure your projects meet stringent federal security requirements confidently and precisely.

- **Students and Educators:** Use this book as a comprehensive resource for learning and teaching RMF principles and practices.

"**NIST SP 800-37 Rev 2 Unlocked: Practical Risk Management Framework Implementation Strategies**" is more than just a guide—it's a comprehensive resource designed to help you navigate the complexities of RMF and achieve a resilient security posture for your organization. Invest in your cybersecurity future today and unlock the full potential of the Risk Management Framework with this indispensable handbook.

Mastering CMMC 2.0: A Comprehensive Guide to Implementing Cybersecurity Maturity in Defense Contracting

"Mastering CMMC 2.0: A Comprehensive Guide to Implementing Cybersecurity Maturity in Defense Contracting" is the ultimate resource for IT professionals and organizations seeking to understand and implement the Cybersecurity Maturity Model Certification (CMMC) framework. This book comprehensively explores CMMC 2.0, covering the model's structure, requirements, and best practices for achieving compliance.

Written by a renowned author, this guide offers a wealth of knowledge and practical insights to help you navigate the complexities of CMMC 2.0. From understanding the different maturity levels and their associated practices to conducting gap analyses and developing remediation plans, this book covers all the essential aspects of CMMC compliance.

You'll learn how to:
- Interpret and apply the CMMC 2.0 requirements to your organization
- Assess your current cybersecurity posture and identify gaps
- Develop and implement effective policies, procedures, and controls
- Conduct thorough risk assessments and prioritize remediation efforts
- Prepare for CMMC assessments and maintain continuous compliance
- Integrate CMMC with other cybersecurity frameworks and standards
- Foster a culture of cybersecurity awareness and continuous improvement

Packed with practical tools, such as assessment templates and plan of action and milestones (POA&M) guidance, this book is an indispensable resource for anyone involved in CMMC implementation, from IT professionals and compliance officers to business leaders and government contractors.

Whether you're new to CMMC or looking to enhance your cybersecurity posture, "Mastering CMMC 2.0" will provide you with the knowledge, strategies, and best practices necessary to succeed in the ever-evolving landscape of defense contracting cybersecurity.

Defense Information Systems Agency (DISA) Security Technical Implementation Guides (STIGs): Best Practices for Secure Government and Military Systems

"Defense Information Systems Agency (DISA) Security Technical Implementation Guides (STIGs): Best Practices for Secure Government and Military Systems" is the ultimate resource for IT professionals, government agents, and military personnel responsible for implementing and maintaining secure systems in compliance with DISA STIGs. This comprehensive guide provides in-depth coverage of STIG requirements, best practices, and real-world case studies, empowering readers to navigate the complex landscape of government and military cybersecurity effectively.

Written by a renowned expert with years of experience in cybersecurity and compliance, this book offers a clear and concise approach to understanding and applying STIG guidelines across various technologies and platforms. Readers will gain valuable insights into the STIG development process, the role of automation and tools, and strategies for overcoming common challenges and pitfalls.

The book features detailed explanations of STIG categories and structures, step-by-step guidance on implementing STIGs in diverse operational environments, and best practices for STIG compliance and auditing. It also explores the latest trends and developments in government and military cybersecurity, including the integration of STIGs with emerging frameworks like zero trust architecture and continuous monitoring.

Whether you're a seasoned cybersecurity professional looking to enhance your expertise or a newcomer to the field seeking to build your skills, this book provides the knowledge and tools you need to excel in your role and contribute to the mission of securing our nation's critical assets and infrastructure.

With its comprehensive coverage, practical insights, and real-world examples, "Defense Information Systems Agency (DISA) Security Technical Implementation Guides (STIGs): Best Practices for Secure Government and Military Systems" is an indispensable resource for anyone involved in government and military cybersecurity. Don't miss this opportunity to elevate your skills, advance your career, and make a lasting impact on the security of our nation's most sensitive systems and data.

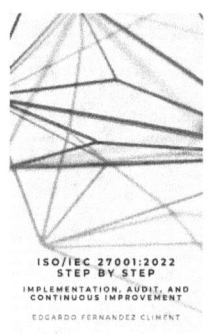

ISO/IEC 27001:2022 Step by Step: Implementation, Audit, and Continuous Improvement

In a world where information security has become a priority for organizations of all sizes, the ISO/IEC 27001:2022 standard emerges as the gold standard for establishing, implementing, maintaining, and continually improving an Information Security Management System (ISMS). "ISO/IEC, 27001:2022 Step by Step" is your definitive guide to understanding and effectively implementing this essential standard.

This book is designed to guide you through the complex ISO/IEC 27001 certification process, breaking down each stage into transparent and manageable steps. From initial planning and risk assessment to implementing security controls and preparing for the certification audit, this book covers everything you need to know to secure your information and achieve certification.

This book offers a deep insight into the standard's requirements and their application in different organizational contexts through detailed explanations, practical examples, and case studies. Additionally, it provides valuable strategies, tips, and tricks to overcome common challenges in implementing and auditing the ISMS.

"ISO/IEC, 27001:2022 Step by Step" is aimed at IT and information security professionals, managers, and those responsible for implementing the standard in their organizations. With a clear focus on continuous improvement, this book is an indispensable tool for keeping your ISMS aligned with best practices and adapted to technological changes and new security threats.

Whether you want to certify your organization for the first time or update your existing ISMS to the latest standard, this book is your perfect companion. It provides expert guidance and the necessary resources to achieve your information security goals.

Mastering ISO/IEC 20000: A Comprehensive Guide to IT Service Management Excellence

Discover the blueprint to IT Service Management (ITSM) excellence with "Mastering ISO/IEC 20000: A Comprehensive Guide to IT Service Management Excellence." This comprehensive guide is designed to navigate professionals through the intricate process of achieving and maintaining ISO/IEC 20000 certification—a quality benchmark in ITSM. Whether you're an IT professional, a manager, or a student of information technology, this book provides a straightforward, structured approach to enhancing your organization's IT services, ensuring they align with business objectives and are fortified with robust cybersecurity measures.

"Mastering ISO/IEC 20000" demystifies the standards of ISO/IEC 20000 and offers readers a deep dive into the practices that lead to successful certification. From the initial steps of gap analysis to the continuous improvement journey beyond certification, this guide is filled with actionable strategies, detailed case studies from various industries, and practical templates to streamline the certification process.

Key features of the book include:
  - A step-by-step roadmap to ISO/IEC 20000 certification, tailored for organizations of any size and sector.
  - In-depth analysis of the integration between ISO/IEC 20000 and other critical standards like ISO/IEC 27001 for information security and ITIL for service management best practices.
  - Practical templates and checklists to guide you in planning, documenting, and managing your ISO/IEC 20000 implementation project.

- A comprehensive glossary of ITSM and ISO/IEC 20000-specific terms to enhance readers' understanding.
- Curated additional resources for further learning, including online materials, training courses, and forums.

Beyond its practical applications, "Mastering ISO/IEC 20000" encourages organizations to view ISO/IEC 20000 certification as a goal and a stepping stone towards establishing a culture of excellence in ITSM. This book is invaluable for anyone looking to elevate their IT service delivery, enhance their cybersecurity posture, and achieve operational excellence in an ever-evolving digital landscape.

Unlock the full potential of your IT services with "Mastering ISO/IEC 20000: Navigating ITSM Excellence." Empower your organization with the knowledge and tools to achieve ITSM excellence and a competitive edge in today's digital world.

www.ingramcontent.com/pod-product-compliance
Lightning Source LLC
Chambersburg PA
CBHW052140220526
45471CB00004B/1458